LOW CHOLESTEROL DIET COOKBOOK FOR BEGINNERS

150 Delicious & Easy Recipes to Support Heart Health and Maintain Wellness. Includes a 45-Day Meal Plan with Weekly Shopping Lists.

Madison Slater

Table of Contents

Copyright Notice 3
Disclaimer 3

Introduction 4
Understanding the Low Cholesterol Diet: A Comprehensive Guide 4
Understanding Good and Bad Cholesterol: A Comprehensive Guide 5
Navigating the Low Cholesterol Diet: Foods to Eat and Avoid for Optimal Health 7

Chapter 1. Breakfast 10
Chapter 2. Snacks and Appetizers 30
Chapter 3. Fish and Seafood 40
Chapter 4. Meat Dishes: Poultry and Beef 55
Chapter 5. Sides and Vegetables 75
Chapter 6. Soups 90
Chapter 7. Salads 100
Chapter 8. Vegetarian Mains 110
Chapter 9. Desserts 130
Chapter 10. Beverages and Smoothies 145
Chapter 11. Staples, Sauces, Dips, and Dressings 150

45-Day Meal Plan and Shopping List 158
Appendix 1. Measurement Conversion Chart 168
Appendix 2. Recipe Index 170

Copyright Notice

© 2024 Madison Slater. All rights reserved.

No part of this publication may be reproduced, distributed, or transmitted in any form or by any means, including photocopying, recording, or other electronic or mechanical methods, without the prior written permission of the author, except in the case of brief quotations embodied in critical reviews and certain other noncommercial uses permitted by copyright law. For permission requests, write to the author at the contact information provided in this book.

Disclaimer

The information provided in this cookbook is for general informational purposes only. All recipes and nutritional advice included in this book are intended to be used as a guide and should not replace the advice of a licensed healthcare professional. While the author has made every effort to ensure the accuracy of the information provided, they make no representations or warranties of any kind about the completeness, accuracy, reliability, suitability, or availability with respect to the content contained in the book for any purpose.

The author is not a medical professional, and the content should not be taken as medical advice. Always consult with a qualified healthcare provider before beginning any diet or exercise program, or making any changes to your health routine. The author disclaims any liability for any loss, damage, or injury that may occur as a result of the use of the information contained in this book.

Individual results may vary. The author does not assume and hereby disclaims any liability to any party for any loss, damage, or disruption caused by errors or omissions, whether such errors or omissions result from negligence, accident, or any other cause.

INTRODUCTION

Understanding the Low Cholesterol Diet: A Comprehensive Guide

The Low Cholesterol Diet is more than just a way of eating; it's a holistic approach to health and wellness. This diet focuses on reducing the intake of foods that can raise cholesterol levels while emphasizing nutrient-dense, heart-healthy choices. Whether you're looking to manage your cholesterol levels, improve your overall health, or simply adopt a more mindful way of eating, the Low Cholesterol Diet offers a path to a healthier lifestyle.

Core Components of the Low Cholesterol Diet
The Low Cholesterol Diet is built around key principles that promote heart health. Here are the core components:

1. **Healthy Fats:** Replace saturated and trans fats with healthier options such as monounsaturated and polyunsaturated fats. Sources include olive oil, avocados, nuts, and seeds.
2. **Fiber-Rich Foods:** Incorporate plenty of soluble fiber, found in oats, beans, lentils, fruits, and vegetables. Fiber helps lower cholesterol by binding to it in the digestive system and removing it from the body.
3. **Lean Proteins:** Opt for lean protein sources like poultry, fish, legumes, and tofu. Fish, particularly fatty fish like salmon, mackerel, and sardines, is rich in omega-3 fatty acids, which are beneficial for heart health.
4. **Whole Grains:** Choose whole grains over refined grains. Whole grains like brown rice, quinoa, barley, and whole-wheat products provide more fiber and nutrients.
5. **Fruits and Vegetables:** A diet abundant in fruits and vegetables is essential. These foods are naturally low in fat and calories and high in vitamins, minerals, and antioxidants.
6. **Limit Cholesterol-Rich Foods:** Reduce the consumption of high-cholesterol foods such as red meat, full-fat dairy products, and processed foods.
7. **Moderation and Balance:** Embrace a balanced approach to eating, focusing on portion control and the quality of food consumed.

Health Benefits of the Low Cholesterol Diet

Heart Health
The most significant benefit of the Low Cholesterol Diet is its positive impact on heart health. By reducing the intake of cholesterol-raising foods and incorporating heart-healthy alternatives, you can lower LDL (bad) cholesterol levels and increase HDL (good) cholesterol. This balance reduces the risk of heart disease and stroke.

Weight Management
A diet rich in whole foods, fiber, and healthy fats promotes satiety and helps with weight management. Maintaining a healthy weight is crucial for managing cholesterol levels and overall health.

Longevity
Adopting a Low Cholesterol Diet can contribute to a longer, healthier life. The diet's focus on nutrient-dense foods supports overall well-being and reduces the risk of chronic diseases.

Holistic Health
Beyond heart health, this diet supports overall wellness. The emphasis on fruits, vegetables, and whole grains provides essential nutrients that boost immune function, improve digestion, and enhance energy levels.

Incorporating the Low Cholesterol Diet into Daily Life

Simple Swaps and Tips
- **Cooking Methods:** Use cooking methods like grilling, baking, steaming, and sautéing with minimal oil instead of frying.
- **Smart Substitutes:** Replace butter with olive oil, and opt for low-fat dairy products instead of full-fat versions.
- **Fiber Boost:** Add beans or lentils to salads and soups for an extra fiber boost.

Meal Planning
Plan meals around whole foods. Include a variety of colors and textures to keep meals interesting and nutritious. Preparing meals at home allows for better control over ingredients and cooking methods.

Shopping for Ingredients
Shop the perimeter of the grocery store where fresh produce, lean proteins, and whole grains are typically found. Read labels carefully to avoid processed foods high in saturated fats and added sugars.

Cooking Techniques
Experiment with herbs and spices to enhance the flavor of your dishes without adding extra fat or sodium. Batch cooking and prepping ingredients in advance can make it easier to stick to the diet.

Embracing the Low Cholesterol Diet Lifestyle
The Low Cholesterol Diet is not just about food; it's about adopting a lifestyle that promotes overall well-being. Here are some additional elements to consider:

Regular Physical Activity
Exercise is a crucial component of heart health. Aim for at least 30 minutes of moderate exercise most days of the week. Activities like walking, swimming, cycling, and yoga are excellent options.

Sharing Meals
Eating with family and friends enhances the dining experience and promotes mindful eating. It's an opportunity to share healthy dishes and enjoy the social aspects of meals.

Mindful Eating
Pay attention to what and how you eat. Eat slowly, savor each bite, and listen to your body's hunger and fullness cues. This practice can prevent overeating and promote better digestion.

Conclusion
Embracing the Low Cholesterol Diet is a step towards a healthier, more vibrant life. By focusing on heart-healthy foods, incorporating regular physical activity, and enjoying meals with loved ones, you can improve your well-being and longevity. Start making small, sustainable changes today, and experience the benefits of this wholesome approach to eating. Your heart, body, and mind will thank you.

Understanding Good and Bad Cholesterol: A Comprehensive Guide

Cholesterol often gets a bad reputation, but it plays a crucial role in our body's functioning. Understanding the difference between good and bad cholesterol is essential for maintaining heart health and overall well-being. This article will delve into what cholesterol is, the types of cholesterol, their roles in the body, and how to manage them effectively.

What is Cholesterol?
Cholesterol is a waxy, fat-like substance found in all the cells of the body. It is necessary for producing hormones, vitamin D, and substances that help digest foods. Our body makes all the cholesterol it needs, but cholesterol is also found in some foods.

Types of Cholesterol
Cholesterol travels through the bloodstream on proteins called lipoproteins. The two main types of lipoproteins are:

Low-Density Lipoprotein (LDL) - Bad Cholesterol
LDL is often referred to as "bad" cholesterol. High levels of LDL can lead to a buildup of cholesterol in the arteries, which can form plaque. Plaque is a thick, hard deposit that can clog arteries and make them less flexible. This condition, known as atherosclerosis, can result in heart disease and stroke.

High-Density Lipoprotein (HDL) - Good Cholesterol
HDL is known as "good" cholesterol. HDL helps remove LDL cholesterol from the arteries by transporting it back to the liver, where it is processed and removed from the body. High levels of HDL cholesterol can reduce the risk of heart disease and stroke.

The Roles of LDL and HDL Cholesterol

LDL (Bad) Cholesterol
- **Role in the Body:** LDL carries cholesterol to various parts of the body, where it is used to repair cell membranes and produce hormones.
- **Health Impact:** When there is too much LDL cholesterol, it can build up in the walls of the arteries. Over time, this buildup narrows the arteries and reduces blood flow to vital organs. This can lead to chest pain, heart attacks, and other cardiovascular diseases.

HDL (Good) Cholesterol
- **Role in the Body:** HDL acts as a scavenger, picking up excess cholesterol from the bloodstream and artery walls and returning it to the liver for disposal.
- **Health Impact:** Higher levels of HDL cholesterol are associated with a lower risk of heart disease. HDL helps maintain arterial health by preventing the buildup of LDL cholesterol.

Managing Cholesterol Levels

Diet and Lifestyle

Foods that Lower LDL (Bad) Cholesterol
- **Oats and Barley:** Rich in soluble fiber, which helps reduce LDL levels.
- **Nuts:** Walnuts, almonds, and other nuts can improve cholesterol levels.
- **Fatty Fish:** Salmon, mackerel, and tuna are high in omega-3 fatty acids, which can lower LDL cholesterol.
- **Fruits and Vegetables:** Packed with fiber, vitamins, and antioxidants that promote heart health.
- **Olive Oil:** Contains monounsaturated fats, which can reduce LDL cholesterol levels.

Foods to Avoid or Limit
- **Trans Fats:** Found in many fried and commercially baked products, trans fats increase LDL and decrease HDL cholesterol.
- **Saturated Fats:** High amounts are found in red meat, full-fat dairy products, and certain oils, contributing to higher LDL levels.
- **Cholesterol-Rich Foods:** Limit intake of organ meats, shellfish, and high-fat dairy products.

Physical Activity
Regular exercise can help raise HDL cholesterol while lowering LDL cholesterol and triglycerides. Aim for at least 30 minutes of moderate-intensity exercise most days of the week.

Weight Management
Maintaining a healthy weight can help control cholesterol levels. Losing excess weight can lower LDL cholesterol and increase HDL cholesterol.

Conclusion
Understanding the difference between good and bad cholesterol is vital for maintaining heart health and overall well-being. By adopting a heart-healthy diet, engaging in regular physical activity, managing weight, and, if necessary, taking prescribed medications, you can keep your cholesterol levels in check and reduce the risk of cardiovascular disease. Regular check-ups and being proactive about your health can lead to a longer, healthier life. Embrace these lifestyle changes today to ensure a vibrant and heart-healthy future.

Navigating the Low Cholesterol Diet: Foods to Eat and Avoid for Optimal Health

The Low Cholesterol Diet is a powerful tool for improving heart health and overall wellness. By making informed dietary choices, you can effectively manage your cholesterol levels and support your health goals. This article provides a comprehensive guide to the foods you should include and avoid in your diet, practical tips for meal preparation, and advice on reading food labels to make the best choices.

Foods to Eat on the Low Cholesterol Diet

1. Healthy Fats

Recommended Foods:
- **Olive Oil:** Rich in monounsaturated fats, which can help reduce LDL cholesterol levels.
- **Avocados:** Packed with monounsaturated fats and fiber.
- **Nuts and Seeds:** Almonds, walnuts, chia seeds, and flaxseeds provide healthy fats, protein, and fiber.
- **Fatty Fish:** Salmon, mackerel, sardines, and trout are high in omega-3 fatty acids, which support heart health.

Nutritional Benefits:
- **Heart Health:** These foods help lower LDL cholesterol and raise HDL cholesterol.
- **Energy and Satiety:** Healthy fats provide long-lasting energy and help keep you full.

Tips for Selection and Preparation:
- Use olive oil for cooking and salad dressings.
- Add avocados to salads, sandwiches, or smoothies.
- Snack on a handful of nuts or add them to yogurt and oatmeal.
- Incorporate fatty fish into your meals at least twice a week by grilling, baking, or steaming.

2. Fiber-Rich Foods

Recommended Foods:
- **Oats and Barley:** Whole grains rich in soluble fiber.
- **Beans and Lentils:** Excellent sources of fiber and protein.
- **Fruits:** Apples, oranges, berries, and pears are high in fiber.
- **Vegetables:** Leafy greens, carrots, and broccoli provide essential vitamins and fiber.

Nutritional Benefits:
- **Cholesterol Management:** Soluble fiber helps reduce LDL cholesterol by binding to it in the digestive system.
- **Digestive Health:** Fiber promotes regular bowel movements and gut health.

Tips for Selection and Preparation:
- Start your day with a bowl of oatmeal topped with fruit.
- Add beans or lentils to soups, stews, and salads.
- Snack on fresh fruit or include it in your breakfast and desserts.
- Fill half your plate with vegetables at every meal.

3. Whole Grains

Recommended Foods:
- **Brown Rice:** A nutritious alternative to white rice.
- **Quinoa:** A protein-rich grain that is versatile and easy to cook.
- **Whole-Wheat Products:** Bread, pasta, and cereals made from whole wheat.

Nutritional Benefits:
- **Energy:** Whole grains provide sustained energy through complex carbohydrates.
- **Nutrient-Rich:** They are rich in vitamins, minerals, and fiber.

Tips for Selection and Preparation:
- Substitute white rice with brown rice or quinoa in your meals.
- Choose whole-wheat bread and pasta over refined options.
- Look for cereals with whole grains as the first ingredient.

Foods to Avoid on the Low Cholesterol Diet

1. Trans Fats

Foods to Avoid:
- **Fried Foods:** French fries, doughnuts, and fried chicken.
- **Baked Goods:** Pastries, cookies, and cakes made with hydrogenated oils.
- **Processed Snacks:** Chips and microwave popcorn.

Reasons for Avoidance:
- **Health Risks:** Trans fats increase LDL cholesterol and decrease HDL cholesterol, raising the risk of heart disease.

Practical Tips:
- Choose baked or grilled options instead of fried foods.
- Read labels to avoid hydrogenated oils and trans fats.
- Make homemade versions of snacks using healthier ingredients.

2. Saturated Fats

Foods to Avoid:
- **Red Meat:** Beef, pork, and lamb.
- **Full-Fat Dairy:** Whole milk, cheese, and butter.
- **Processed Meats:** Sausages, bacon, and hot dogs.

Reasons for Avoidance:
- **Cholesterol Levels:** Saturated fats raise LDL cholesterol, increasing the risk of heart disease.

Practical Tips:
- Choose lean meats like poultry and fish.
- Use low-fat or fat-free dairy products.
- Limit consumption of processed meats and opt for fresh alternatives.

3. Cholesterol-Rich Foods

Foods to Avoid:
- **Organ Meats:** Liver and kidneys.
- **Shellfish:** Shrimp and lobster (in large quantities).
- **Egg Yolks:** High in dietary cholesterol.

Reasons for Avoidance:
- **Cholesterol Levels:** These foods can contribute to high LDL cholesterol levels.

Practical Tips:
- Eat organ meats and shellfish in moderation.
- Use egg whites or cholesterol-free egg substitutes.
- Incorporate more plant-based proteins into your diet.

Reading Food Labels

Key Ingredients to Look Out For
- **Trans Fats:** Avoid products with hydrogenated or partially hydrogenated oils.
- **Saturated Fats:** Choose products with low saturated fat content.
- **Cholesterol:** Look for foods with low dietary cholesterol.
- **Fiber:** Aim for high fiber content to support heart health.

Tips for Making Informed Choices
- **Serving Size:** Be mindful of the serving size to accurately assess nutritional content.
- **Ingredients List:** The shorter the list, the better. Avoid foods with added sugars and unhealthy fats.
- **Health Claims:** Be cautious of labels like "low-fat" or "cholesterol-free" and check the actual nutritional content.

Conclusion

Making the shift to a Low Cholesterol Diet can significantly improve your health and well-being. By focusing on heart-healthy foods and avoiding those that can raise cholesterol levels, you can take control of your diet and health. Experiment with new recipes, enjoy the variety of flavors and textures, and embrace this lifestyle change with confidence. Remember, small, consistent changes can lead to significant long-term benefits. Your heart and body will thank you for it.

CHAPTER 1. BREAKFAST

1. Avocado and Spinach Breakfast Wrap

Yield: 2 servings Prepration time: 10 Minutes Cooking Time: 5 Minutes

Nutritional Information (Per Serving):
- Calories: 250
- Protein: 12g
- Carbohydrates: 34g
- Fats: 10g
- Fiber: 8g
- Cholesterol: 0mg
- Sodium: 320mg

Ingredients:

- **Whole Wheat Tortillas:** 2 large
- **Avocado:** 1 ripe, peeled, pitted, and sliced
- **Baby Spinach:** 2 cups, fresh
- **Egg Whites:** 4 large (or 1 cup liquid egg whites)
- **Cherry Tomatoes:** 1/2 cup, halved
- **Red Onion:** 1/4 cup, finely chopped
- **Bell Pepper:** 1/2 cup, diced (any color)
- **Olive Oil:** 1 tsp
- **Fresh Cilantro:** 2 tbsp, chopped (optional)
- **Lemon Juice:** 1 tsp, freshly squeezed
- **Salt:** 1/4 tsp
- **Black Pepper:** 1/4 tsp
- **Low-Fat Greek Yogurt:** 2 tbsp (optional, for garnish)
- **Hot Sauce:** To taste (optional)

Customizable Ingredients or Garnishes:
- **Sliced Jalapeños:** For added spice
- **Fresh Salsa:** For additional flavor
- **Grated Low-Fat Cheese:** 2 tbsp (optional, for extra creaminess)

Instructions:

1. **Prepare the Ingredients:**
   - Slice the avocado, chop the vegetables, and halve the cherry tomatoes.
   - In a small bowl, whisk the egg whites with a pinch of salt and pepper.
2. **Cook the Vegetables:**
   - In a non-stick skillet, heat 1 tsp of olive oil over medium heat.
   - Add the chopped red onion and bell pepper to the skillet. Sauté for 2-3 minutes until they begin to soften.
3. **Cook the Egg Whites:**
   - Add the whisked egg whites to the skillet with the vegetables.
   - Cook, stirring gently, until the egg whites are fully cooked and slightly scrambled, about 3-4 minutes.
   - Add the baby spinach and cherry tomatoes to the skillet. Cook for an additional 1-2 minutes until the spinach wilts slightly.
   - Remove from heat.
4. **Assemble the Wraps:**
   - Lay the whole wheat tortillas flat on a clean surface.
   - Divide the egg white and vegetable mixture evenly between the two tortillas, placing the mixture in the center of each tortilla.
   - Top with sliced avocado, fresh cilantro, and a drizzle of lemon juice.
5. **Wrap and Serve:**
   - Fold in the sides of each tortilla, then roll them up from the bottom to form a wrap.
   - Slice the wraps in half if desired and serve immediately.
6. **Optional Garnishes:**
   - Serve with a dollop of low-fat Greek yogurt and a dash of hot sauce on the side.

2. Quinoa and Berry Breakfast Bowl

Yield: 2 servings Prepration time: 10 Minutes Cooking Time: 20 Minutes

Ingredients:

- **Quinoa:** 1/2 cup, uncooked
- **Water:** 1 cup
- **Fresh Berries:** 1 cup (e.g., blueberries, strawberries, raspberries, blackberries)
- **Banana:** 1, sliced
- **Almond Milk:** 1 cup, unsweetened
- **Chia Seeds:** 1 tbsp
- **Maple Syrup:** 1 tbsp (optional)
- **Vanilla Extract:** 1/2 tsp
- **Cinnamon:** 1/4 tsp
- **Nutmeg:** 1/8 tsp
- **Fresh Mint:** 1 tbsp, chopped (optional, for garnish)

Nutritional Information (Per Serving):
- **Calories:** 320
- **Protein:** 8g
- **Carbohydrates:** 55g
- **Fats:** 8g
- **Fiber:** 9g
- **Cholesterol:** 0mg
- **Sodium:** 50mg

Customizable Ingredients or Garnishes:
- **Sliced Almonds:** 2 tbsp
- **Pumpkin Seeds:** 1 tbsp
- **Coconut Flakes:** 1 tbsp, unsweetened
- **Flaxseeds:** 1 tbsp, ground

Instructions:

1. **Cook the Quinoa:**
   - Rinse the quinoa under cold water to remove any bitterness.
   - In a medium saucepan, bring 1 cup of water to a boil.
   - Add the rinsed quinoa to the boiling water. Reduce the heat to low, cover, and simmer for about 15 minutes or until the quinoa is tender and the water is absorbed.
   - Once cooked, fluff the quinoa with a fork and let it cool slightly.
2. **Prepare the Almond Milk Mixture:**
   - In a small bowl, combine the almond milk, chia seeds, maple syrup (if using), vanilla extract, cinnamon, and nutmeg. Mix well.
   - Let the mixture sit for about 5 minutes to allow the chia seeds to thicken the milk slightly.
3. **Assemble the Breakfast Bowl:**
   - Divide the cooked quinoa evenly between two bowls.
   - Pour the almond milk mixture over the quinoa in each bowl.
   - Top each bowl with the fresh berries and banana slices.
4. **Add Customizable Garnishes:**
   - Sprinkle sliced almonds, pumpkin seeds, and unsweetened coconut flakes on top, if desired.
   - Garnish with fresh mint for an extra burst of flavor.
5. **Serve:**
   - Serve immediately, or cover and refrigerate for a chilled breakfast option.

3. Egg White Veggie Omelette

Yield: 2 servings *Preparation time: 10 Minutes* *Cooking Time: 10 Minutes*

Ingredients:

- **Egg Whites:** 6 large (or 3/4 cup liquid egg whites)
- **Spinach:** 1 cup, fresh
- **Bell Pepper:** 1/2 cup, diced (any color)
- **Red Onion:** 1/4 cup, finely chopped
- **Cherry Tomatoes:** 1/2 cup, halved
- **Mushrooms:** 1/2 cup, sliced
- **Olive Oil:** 1 tsp
- **Garlic:** 1 clove, minced
- **Salt:** 1/4 tsp
- **Black Pepper:** 1/4 tsp
- **Fresh Parsley:** 1 tbsp, chopped (optional)
- **Avocado:** 1/2, sliced (optional, for garnish)
- **Low-Fat Cheese:** 2 tbsp, shredded (optional)

Nutritional Information (Per Serving):
- **Calories:** 180
- **Protein:** 16g
- **Carbohydrates:** 10g
- **Fats:** 7g
- **Fiber:** 3g
- **Cholesterol:** 0mg
- **Sodium:** 320mg

Customizable Ingredients or Garnishes:
- **Sliced Jalapeños:** For added spice
- **Fresh Salsa:** For additional flavor
- **Hot Sauce:** To taste
- **Whole Wheat Toast:** 1 slice per serving, optional

Instructions:

1. **Prepare the Ingredients:**
   - Dice the bell pepper, chop the red onion, halve the cherry tomatoes, and slice the mushrooms.
   - In a small bowl, whisk the egg whites with a pinch of salt and pepper.
2. **Cook the Vegetables:**
   - In a non-stick skillet, heat 1 tsp of olive oil over medium heat.
   - Add the minced garlic and cook for 30 seconds until fragrant.
   - Add the red onion, bell pepper, mushrooms, and cherry tomatoes to the skillet. Sauté for 3-4 minutes until the vegetables are tender.
   - Add the fresh spinach and cook for an additional 1-2 minutes until wilted. Remove the vegetable mixture from the skillet and set aside.
3. **Cook the Egg Whites:**
   - In the same skillet, pour the whisked egg whites, spreading them evenly to cover the bottom of the skillet.
   - Cook over medium heat for 2-3 minutes until the egg whites begin to set.
4. **Assemble the Omelette:**
   - Once the egg whites are mostly set, add the cooked vegetable mixture to one half of the omelette.
   - If using, sprinkle the shredded low-fat cheese over the vegetables.
   - Carefully fold the other half of the omelette over the filling.
5. **Finish Cooking:**
   - Cook for an additional 1-2 minutes until the egg whites are fully cooked and the cheese (if used) is melted.
6. **Serve:**
   - Transfer the omelette to a plate.
   - Garnish with fresh parsley and avocado slices, if desired.
   - Serve immediately, optionally with a slice of whole wheat toast on the side.

4. Whole Grain Banana Pancakes

Yield: 4 servings Prepration time: 10 Minutes Cooking Time: 15 Minutes

Ingredients:

- **Whole Wheat Flour:** 1 cup
- **Rolled Oats:** 1/2 cup
- **Baking Powder:** 2 tsp
- **Baking Soda:** 1/2 tsp
- **Salt:** 1/4 tsp
- **Cinnamon:** 1/2 tsp
- **Nutmeg:** 1/4 tsp
- **Bananas:** 2 ripe, mashed
- **Almond Milk:** 1 cup, unsweetened
- **Egg Whites:** 2 large (or 1/4 cup liquid egg whites)
- **Vanilla Extract:** 1 tsp
- **Olive Oil:** 1 tbsp (or melted coconut oil)
- **Honey or Maple Syrup:** 1 tbsp (optional)

Nutritional Information (Per Serving):
- **Calories:** 220
- **Protein:** 6g
- **Carbohydrates:** 38g
- **Fats:** 6g
- **Fiber:** 5g
- **Cholesterol:** 0mg
- **Sodium:** 280mg

Customizable Ingredients or Garnishes:
- **Fresh Berries:** 1 cup
- **Sliced Almonds:** 2 tbsp
- **Chopped Walnuts:** 2 tbsp
- **Chia Seeds:** 1 tbsp
- **Unsweetened Coconut Flakes:** 2 tbsp
- **Additional Banana Slices:** For topping
- **Greek Yogurt:** 1/4 cup, low-fat (optional)
- **Maple Syrup or Honey:** For drizzling

Instructions:

1. **Prepare the Dry Ingredients:**
   - In a large bowl, combine the whole wheat flour, rolled oats, baking powder, baking soda, salt, cinnamon, and nutmeg. Mix well.
2. **Prepare the Wet Ingredients:**
   - In a separate bowl, mash the ripe bananas until smooth.
   - Add the almond milk, egg whites, vanilla extract, and olive oil (or melted coconut oil) to the mashed bananas. Mix well.
3. **Combine Wet and Dry Ingredients:**
   - Pour the wet ingredients into the bowl with the dry ingredients.
   - Stir until just combined. Be careful not to overmix; a few lumps are okay.
4. **Cook the Pancakes:**
   - Heat a non-stick skillet or griddle over medium heat. Lightly coat with cooking spray or a small amount of olive oil.
   - Pour 1/4 cup of batter onto the skillet for each pancake. Spread the batter out slightly with the back of a spoon.
   - Cook until bubbles form on the surface of the pancakes and the edges start to look set, about 2-3 minutes.
   - Flip the pancakes and cook for another 2-3 minutes, until golden brown and cooked through.
   - Repeat with the remaining batter, adding more cooking spray or oil as needed.
5. **Serve:**
   - Stack the pancakes on plates.
   - Top with fresh berries, sliced almonds, chopped walnuts, chia seeds, unsweetened coconut flakes, and additional banana slices as desired.
   - Serve with a dollop of low-fat Greek yogurt and a drizzle of maple syrup or honey, if using.

5. Chia Seed Pudding with Fresh Berries

Yield: 4 servings • Prepration time: 10 Minutes • Cooking Time: 0 Minutes • Chilling Time: 4 hours (or overnight)

Ingredients:

- **Chia Seeds:** 1/2 cup
- **Unsweetened Almond Milk:** 2 cups
- **Maple Syrup:** 2 tbsp (optional)
- **Vanilla Extract:** 1 tsp
- **Cinnamon:** 1/2 tsp (optional)
- **Fresh Berries:** 2 cups (e.g., strawberries, blueberries, raspberries, blackberries)
- **Sliced Almonds:** 1/4 cup (optional, for garnish)
- **Unsweetened Coconut Flakes:** 2 tbsp (optional, for garnish)
- **Fresh Mint:** 1 tbsp, chopped (optional, for garnish)

Nutritional Information (Per Serving):
- **Calories:** 180
- **Protein:** 5g
- **Carbohydrates:** 25g
- **Fats:** 8g
- **Fiber:** 10g
- **Cholesterol:** 0mg
- **Sodium:** 90mg

Customizable Ingredients or Garnishes:
- **Sliced Banana:** 1
- **Chopped Nuts:** 2 tbsp (e.g., walnuts, pecans)
- **Coconut Yogurt:** 1/2 cup
- **Cacao Nibs:** 1 tbsp

Instructions:

1. **Prepare the Chia Seed Mixture:**
   - In a medium bowl, combine the chia seeds, almond milk, maple syrup (if using), vanilla extract, and cinnamon (if using).
   - Stir well to ensure the chia seeds are evenly distributed and not clumping together.
2. **Chill the Pudding:**
   - Cover the bowl and refrigerate for at least 4 hours, or overnight, to allow the chia seeds to absorb the liquid and form a pudding-like consistency.
   - Stir the mixture once or twice during the first hour to prevent clumping.
3. **Prepare the Fresh Berries:**
   - Wash and slice the fresh berries if needed.
   - Set aside until ready to serve.
4. **Assemble the Pudding:**
   - Once the chia seed pudding has thickened, give it a good stir.
   - Divide the pudding evenly into four serving bowls or jars.
5. **Add Toppings:**
   - Top each serving with fresh berries.
   - Add optional garnishes such as sliced almonds, unsweetened coconut flakes, sliced banana, chopped nuts, coconut yogurt, or cacao nibs as desired.
6. **Serve:**
   - Garnish with fresh mint if using and serve immediately, or cover and refrigerate until ready to eat.

6. Low-Fat Greek Yogurt Parfait

Yield: 2 servings *Prepration time: 10 Minutes* *Cooking Time: 0 Minutes*

Ingredients:

- **Low-Fat Greek Yogurt:** 2 cups
- **Granola:** 1/2 cup (choose a low-sugar variety)
- **Fresh Berries:** 1 cup (e.g., blueberries, strawberries, raspberries)
- **Honey:** 1 tbsp (optional)
- **Chia Seeds:** 1 tbsp
- **Fresh Mint:** 1 tbsp, chopped (optional, for garnish)

Nutritional Information (Per Serving):
- **Calories:** 220
- **Protein:** 15g
- **Carbohydrates:** 28g
- **Fats:** 6g
- **Fiber:** 5g
- **Cholesterol:** 5mg
- **Sodium:** 85mg

Customizable Ingredients or Garnishes:
- **Sliced Banana:** 1
- **Chopped Nuts:** 2 tbsp (e.g., almonds, walnuts)
- **Unsweetened Coconut Flakes:** 2 tbsp

Instructions:

1. **Layer the Parfait:**
   - In two glasses or bowls, layer 1/4 cup of granola at the bottom.
   - Add 1/2 cup of low-fat Greek yogurt over the granola.
   - Add a layer of fresh berries.
   - Repeat the layers until all ingredients are used, finishing with a layer of berries on top.
2. **Add Garnishes:**
   - Drizzle honey over the top, if using.
   - Sprinkle chia seeds over the parfait.
   - Add any optional garnishes such as chopped nuts or unsweetened coconut flakes.
3. **Serve:**
   - Garnish with fresh mint if desired and serve immediately.

7. Almond Butter and Banana Smoothie Bowl

Yield: 2 servings Prepration time: 10 Minutes Cooking Time: 0 Minutes

Nutritional Information (Per Serving):
- **Calories:** 320
- **Protein:** 8g
- **Carbohydrates:** 42g
- **Fats:** 14g
- **Fiber:** 9g
- **Cholesterol:** 0mg
- **Sodium:** 110mg

Ingredients:

- **Frozen Banana:** 2, sliced
- **Almond Milk:** 1 cup, unsweetened
- **Almond Butter:** 2 tbsp
- **Spinach:** 1 cup, fresh
- **Chia Seeds:** 1 tbsp
- **Fresh Banana:** 1, sliced (for topping)
- **Granola:** 1/4 cup (for topping)
- **Fresh Berries:** 1/2 cup (for topping)

Customizable Ingredients or Garnishes:
- **Coconut Flakes:** 2 tbsp
- **Sliced Almonds:** 2 tbsp
- **Pumpkin Seeds:** 1 tbsp

Instructions:

1. **Blend the Smoothie:**
   - In a blender, combine the frozen banana, almond milk, almond butter, spinach, and chia seeds.
   - Blend until smooth and creamy.
2. **Assemble the Smoothie Bowl:**
   - Divide the smoothie mixture between two bowls.
   - Top with fresh banana slices, granola, and fresh berries.
3. **Add Garnishes:**
   - Add any optional garnishes such as coconut flakes, sliced almonds, or pumpkin seeds.
4. **Serve:**
   - Serve immediately.

8. Oatmeal with Fresh Apples and Cinnamon

Yield: 2 servings   Prepration time: 5 Minutes   Cooking Time: 10 Minutes

Nutritional Information (Per Serving):
- Calories: 250
- Protein: 6g
- Carbohydrates: 42g
- Fats: 8g
- Fiber: 7g
- Cholesterol: 0mg
- Sodium: 10mg

Ingredients:

- **Rolled Oats:** 1 cup
- **Water:** 2 cups
- **Apple:** 1, chopped
- **Cinnamon:** 1 tsp
- **Maple Syrup:** 1 tbsp (optional)
- **Chopped Walnuts:** 2 tbsp
- **Chia Seeds:** 1 tbsp

Customizable Ingredients or Garnishes:
- **Fresh Berries:** 1/2 cup
- **Sliced Banana:** 1
- **Unsweetened Coconut Flakes:** 2 tbsp

Instructions:

1. **Cook the Oatmeal:**
   - In a medium saucepan, bring water to a boil.
   - Add the rolled oats and reduce heat to a simmer.
   - Cook for about 5 minutes, stirring occasionally.
2. **Add Apples and Cinnamon:**
   - Add the chopped apple and cinnamon to the saucepan.
   - Cook for another 3-4 minutes until the apples are tender.
3. **Sweeten (Optional):**
   - Stir in maple syrup if using.
4. **Serve:**
   - Divide the oatmeal between two bowls.
   - Top with chopped walnuts and chia seeds.
   - Add any optional garnishes such as fresh berries, sliced banana, or coconut flakes.

9. Veggie-Packed Breakfast Frittata

Yield: 4 servings   Prepration time: 15 Minutes   Cooking Time: 20 Minutes

Nutritional Information (Per Serving):
- Calories: 120
- Protein: 12g
- Carbohydrates: 6g
- Fats: 4g
- Fiber: 2g
- Cholesterol: 0mg
- Sodium: 220mg

Ingredients:

- **Egg Whites:** 8 large (or 1 cup liquid egg whites)
- **Spinach:** 2 cups, fresh
- **Bell Pepper:** 1/2 cup, diced (any color)
- **Cherry Tomatoes:** 1/2 cup, halved
- **Red Onion:** 1/4 cup, finely chopped
- **Mushrooms:** 1/2 cup, sliced
- **Olive Oil:** 1 tsp
- **Garlic:** 1 clove, minced
- **Salt:** 1/4 tsp
- **Black Pepper:** 1/4 tsp
- **Fresh Herbs:** 1 tbsp, chopped (e.g., parsley, basil)

Customizable Ingredients or Garnishes:
- **Low-Fat Cheese:** 1/4 cup, shredded
- **Sliced Avocado:** 1/2, for topping
- **Hot Sauce:** To taste

Instructions:

1. **Preheat the Oven:**
   - Preheat the oven to 375°F (190°C).
2. **Cook the Vegetables:**
   - In an oven-safe skillet, heat the olive oil over medium heat.
   - Add the minced garlic and cook for 30 seconds until fragrant.
   - Add the red onion, bell pepper, mushrooms, and cherry tomatoes. Sauté for 3-4 minutes until the vegetables are tender.
   - Add the fresh spinach and cook for an additional 1-2 minutes until wilted.
   - Season with salt and black pepper.
3. **Prepare the Egg Whites:**
   - In a medium bowl, whisk the egg whites until slightly frothy.
   - Pour the egg whites over the cooked vegetables in the skillet.
   - Stir gently to combine.
4. **Bake the Frittata:**
   - Transfer the skillet to the preheated oven.
   - Bake for 15-20 minutes, or until the egg whites are set and the frittata is lightly golden on top.
5. **Serve:**
   - Remove from the oven and let it cool slightly.
   - Sprinkle with fresh herbs and any optional garnishes like shredded low-fat cheese or sliced avocado.
   - Slice into wedges and serve.

10. Smoked Salmon and Avocado Toast

Yield: 2 servings Prepration time: 10 Minutes Cooking Time: 0 Minutes

Ingredients:

- **Whole Grain Bread:** 2 slices
- **Avocado:** 1 ripe, mashed
- **Smoked Salmon:** 4 oz, thinly sliced
- **Lemon Juice:** 1 tsp
- **Salt:** 1/4 tsp
- **Black Pepper:** 1/4 tsp
- **Red Onion:** 1/4 cup, thinly sliced
- **Capers:** 1 tbsp (optional)
- **Fresh Dill:** 1 tbsp, chopped (optional, for garnish)

Nutritional Information (Per Serving):
- **Calories:** 250
- **Protein:** 15g
- **Carbohydrates:** 20g
- **Fats:** 14g
- **Fiber:** 6g
- **Cholesterol:** 20mg
- **Sodium:** 480mg

Customizable Ingredients or Garnishes:
- **Cherry Tomatoes:** 1/2 cup, halved
- **Radish Slices:** 1/4 cup
- **Cucumber Slices:** 1/4 cup

Instructions:

1. **Toast the Bread:**
   - Toast the whole grain bread slices until golden and crispy.
2. **Prepare the Avocado:**
   - In a small bowl, mash the avocado with lemon juice, salt, and black pepper.
3. **Assemble the Toast:**
   - Spread the mashed avocado evenly over the toasted bread slices.
   - Top each slice with smoked salmon.
   - Add thinly sliced red onion and capers if using.
4. **Serve:**
   - Garnish with fresh dill and any optional toppings like cherry tomatoes, radish slices, or cucumber slices.
   - Serve immediately.

11. Blueberry Almond Overnight Oats

Yield: 2 servings | Prepration time: 5 Minutes | Cooking Time: 0 Minutes (overnight refrigeration)

Ingredients:

- **Rolled Oats:** 1 cup
- **Unsweetened Almond Milk:** 1 cup
- **Chia Seeds:** 1 tbsp
- **Maple Syrup:** 1 tbsp (optional)
- **Vanilla Extract:** 1 tsp
- **Blueberries:** 1 cup, fresh or frozen ((e.g., strawberries, raspberries)
- **Almonds:** 2 tbsp, sliced
- **Cinnamon:** 1/2 tsp

Nutritional Information (Per Serving):
- **Calories:** 260
- **Protein:** 7g
- **Carbohydrates:** 40g
- **Fats:** 9g
- **Fiber:** 8g
- **Cholesterol:** 0mg
- **Sodium:** 50mg

Instructions:

1. **Prepare the Oats:**
   - In a medium bowl, combine rolled oats, almond milk, chia seeds, maple syrup (if using), and vanilla extract.
   - Stir well to combine.
2. **Add the Blueberries:**
   - Fold in the blueberries.
3. **Refrigerate:**
   - Cover the bowl and refrigerate overnight or for at least 4 hours.
4. **Serve:**
   - In the morning, give the oats a good stir and divide between two bowls.
   - Top with sliced almonds and a sprinkle of cinnamon.
   - Add any customizable ingredients or garnishes as desired.

12. Spinach and Mushroom Breakfast Tacos

Yield: 4 servings (2 tacos per serving) | **Prepration time:** 10 Minutes | **Cooking Time:** 15 Minutes

Ingredients:

- **Corn Tortillas:** 8
- **Egg Whites:** 8 large (or 1 cup liquid egg whites)
- **Spinach:** 2 cups, fresh
- **Mushrooms:** 1 cup, sliced
- **Olive Oil:** 1 tbsp
- **Garlic:** 1 clove, minced
- **Salt:** 1/4 tsp
- **Black Pepper:** 1/4 tsp
- **Avocado:** 1, sliced
- **Salsa:** 1/2 cup

Nutritional Information (Per Serving):
- Calories: 230
- Protein: 15g
- Carbohydrates: 28g
- Fats: 9g
- Fiber: 8g
- Cholesterol: 0mg
- Sodium: 300mg

Instructions:

1. **Prepare the Vegetables:**
   - In a skillet, heat olive oil over medium heat.
   - Add minced garlic and cook for 30 seconds.
   - Add mushrooms and cook for 5 minutes until softened.
   - Add spinach and cook until wilted, about 2 minutes.
   - Season with salt and pepper and set aside.
2. **Cook the Egg Whites:**
   - In a separate skillet, cook the egg whites over medium heat, stirring frequently until fully cooked.
3. **Assemble the Tacos:**
   - Warm the corn tortillas.
   - Divide the egg whites among the tortillas.
   - Top with the spinach and mushroom mixture.
   - Add slices of avocado and a spoonful of salsa.
4. **Serve:**
   - Serve immediately.

13. Baked Sweet Potato and Black Bean Breakfast Skillet

Yield: 4 servings   Prepration time: 10 Minutes   Cooking Time: 30 Minutes

Nutritional Information (Per Serving):
- Calories: 310
- Protein: 7g
- Carbohydrates: 48g
- Fats: 12g
- Fiber: 12g
- Cholesterol: 0mg
- Sodium: 420mg

Ingredients:

- **Sweet Potatoes:** 2 large, peeled and diced
- **Black Beans:** 1 can (15 oz), drained and rinsed
- **Red Bell Pepper:** 1, diced
- **Red Onion:** 1, diced
- **Olive Oil:** 2 tbsp
- **Cumin:** 1 tsp
- **Paprika:** 1 tsp
- **Salt:** 1/2 tsp
- **Black Pepper:** 1/4 tsp
- **Avocado:** 1, sliced
- **Cilantro:** 2 tbsp, chopped

Instructions:

1. **Preheat the Oven:**
   - Preheat oven to 400°F (200°C).
2. **Prepare the Vegetables:**
   - In a large mixing bowl, toss sweet potatoes, bell pepper, and red onion with olive oil, cumin, paprika, salt, and black pepper.
3. **Bake the Vegetables:**
   - Spread the vegetable mixture evenly on a baking sheet.
   - Bake for 25-30 minutes, or until the sweet potatoes are tender and slightly crispy.
4. **Add the Black Beans:**
   - Remove from the oven and add the black beans.
   - Return to the oven for an additional 5 minutes to heat the beans through.
5. **Serve:**
   - Divide the mixture into four bowls.
   - Top with avocado slices and chopped cilantro.

14. Low-Fat Cottage Cheese and Fresh Fruit

Yield: 2 servings   Prepration time: 5 Minutes   Cooking Time: 0 Minutes

Nutritional Information (Per Serving):
- **Calories:** 180
- **Protein:** 15g
- **Carbohydrates:** 28g
- **Fats:** 2g
- **Fiber:** 5g
- **Cholesterol:** 10mg
- **Sodium:** 400mg

Ingredients:

- **Low-Fat Cottage Cheese:** 1 cup
- **Fresh Berries:** 1 cup (e.g., blueberries, strawberries, raspberries)
- **Sliced Banana:** 1
- **Honey:** 1 tbsp (optional)
- **Chia Seeds:** 1 tbsp

Instructions:

1. **Prepare the Fruit:**
   - Wash the berries and slice the banana.
2. **Assemble the Dish:**
   - Divide the cottage cheese between two bowls.
   - Top with fresh berries and banana slices.
   - Drizzle with honey if using.
   - Sprinkle chia seeds on top.
3. **Serve:**
   - Serve immediately.

15. Turkey and Avocado Breakfast Sandwich

Yield: 2 servings   Prepration time: 10 Minutes   Cooking Time: 5 Minutes

Ingredients:

- **Whole Grain English Muffins:** 2, split and toasted
- **Turkey Breast:** 4 slices, cooked
- **Avocado:** 1, sliced
- **Tomato:** 1, sliced
- **Spinach:** 1 cup, fresh
- **Mustard:** 2 tsp (optional)

Nutritional Information (Per Serving):
- **Calories:** 300
- **Protein:** 20g
- **Carbohydrates:** 32g
- **Fats:** 12g
- **Fiber:** 8g
- **Cholesterol:** 30mg
- **Sodium:** 500mg

Instructions:

1. **Toast the Muffins:**
   - Split and toast the English muffins.
2. **Assemble the Sandwiches:**
   - On the bottom half of each muffin, layer slices of turkey, avocado, tomato, and spinach.
   - Add mustard if using.
   - Top with the other half of the muffin.
3. **Serve:**
   - Serve immediately.

16. Apple Cinnamon Quinoa Porridge

Yield: 2 servings Prepration time: 5 Minutes Cooking Time: 15 Minutes

Ingredients:

- **Quinoa:** 1/2 cup, uncooked
- **Water:** 1 cup
- **Apple:** 1, chopped
- **Cinnamon:** 1 tsp
- **Maple Syrup:** 1 tbsp (optional)
- **Chopped Walnuts:** 2 tbsp
- **Chia Seeds:** 1 tbsp

Nutritional Information (Per Serving):
- Calories: 250
- Protein: 6g
- Carbohydrates: 40g
- Fats: 8g
- Fiber: 6g
- Cholesterol: 0mg
- Sodium: 10mg
- Potassium: 250mg

Instructions:

1. **Cook the Quinoa:**
   - In a medium saucepan, bring water to a boil.
   - Add quinoa and reduce heat to a simmer.
   - Cook for about 12 minutes, or until quinoa is tender and water is absorbed.
2. **Add Apple and Cinnamon:**
   - Add chopped apple and cinnamon to the saucepan.
   - Cook for another 3 minutes until the apple is tender.
3. **Sweeten (Optional):**
   - Stir in maple syrup if using.
4. **Serve:**
   - Divide the quinoa porridge between two bowls.
   - Top with chopped walnuts and chia seeds.

17. Savory Oatmeal with Poached Egg

Yield: 2 servings • Prepration time: 5 Minutes • Cooking Time: 15 Minutes

Nutritional Information (Per Serving):
- Calories: 220
- Protein: 12g
- Carbohydrates: 28g
- Fats: 8g
- Fiber: 5g
- Cholesterol: 0mg
- Sodium: 200mg
- Potassium: 450mg

Ingredients:

- **Rolled Oats:** 1 cup
- **Water:** 2 cups
- **Spinach:** 1 cup, fresh
- **Garlic:** 1 clove, minced
- **Olive Oil:** 1 tsp
- **Salt:** 1/4 tsp
- **Black Pepper:** 1/4 tsp
- **Eggs:** 2 large
- **White Vinegar:** 1 tbsp
- **Chopped Chives:** 2 tbsp (optional)
- **Parmesan Cheese:** 2 tbsp, grated (optional)

Instructions:

1. **Cook the Oatmeal:**
   - In a medium saucepan, bring water to a boil.
   - Add rolled oats, reduce heat, and simmer for about 5 minutes, stirring occasionally.
2. **Sauté the Spinach:**
   - In a small skillet, heat olive oil over medium heat.
   - Add minced garlic and cook for 30 seconds.
   - Add spinach and cook until wilted, about 2 minutes.
   - Season with salt and black pepper.
3. **Poach the Eggs:**
   - In a small saucepan, bring water to a gentle simmer.
   - Add white vinegar.
   - Crack each egg into a small bowl and gently slide it into the simmering water.
   - Poach for about 3-4 minutes until the whites are set but the yolks are still runny.
   - Remove with a slotted spoon and drain on paper towels.
4. **Assemble the Dish:**
   - Divide the cooked oatmeal between two bowls.
   - Top each bowl with sautéed spinach and a poached egg.
   - Sprinkle with chopped chives and grated Parmesan cheese if using.

18. Whole Wheat English Muffin with Tomato and Basil

Yield: 2 servings   Prepration time: 5 Minutes   Cooking Time: 5 Minutes

Nutritional Information (Per Serving):
- Calories: 180
- Protein: 5g
- Carbohydrates: 28g
- Fats: 7g
- Fiber: 6g
- Cholesterol: 0mg
- Sodium: 300mg
- Potassium: 400mg

Ingredients:

- **Whole Wheat English Muffins:** 2, split and toasted
- **Tomato:** 1 large, sliced
- **Fresh Basil Leaves:** 8-10 leaves
- **Olive Oil:** 2 tsp
- **Salt:** 1/4 tsp
- **Black Pepper:** 1/4 tsp
- **Balsamic Glaze:** 1 tsp (optional)

Instructions:

1. **Toast the Muffins:**
   - Split and toast the whole wheat English muffins.
2. **Prepare the Toppings:**
   - Slice the tomato and wash the basil leaves.
3. **Assemble the Muffins:**
   - Place tomato slices on each toasted muffin half.
   - Top with fresh basil leaves.
   - Drizzle with olive oil and sprinkle with salt and black pepper.
   - Add a drizzle of balsamic glaze if using.
4. **Serve:**
   - Serve immediately.

19. Green Smoothie with Kale and Pineapple

Yield: 2 servings   Prepration time: 5 Minutes   Cooking Time: 0 Minutes

Ingredients:

- **Kale:** 2 cups, chopped
- **Pineapple:** 1 cup, diced (fresh or frozen)
- **Banana:** 1, sliced
- **Unsweetened Almond Milk:** 1 cup
- **Chia Seeds:** 1 tbsp
- **Lemon Juice:** 1 tbsp
- **Ice Cubes:** 1/2 cup (optional)

Nutritional Information (Per Serving):
- **Calories:** 160
- **Protein:** 3g
- **Carbohydrates:** 35g
- **Fats:** 3g
- **Fiber:** 6g
- **Cholesterol:** 0mg
- **Sodium:** 50mg
- **Potassium:** 500mg

Instructions:

1. **Blend the Smoothie:**
   - In a blender, combine kale, pineapple, banana, almond milk, chia seeds, lemon juice, and ice cubes if using.
   - Blend until smooth and creamy.
2. **Serve:**
   - Pour into two glasses and serve immediately.

20. Ricotta and Berry Stuffed French Toast

Yield: 2 servings Prepration time: 10 Minutes Cooking Time: 10 Minutes

Ingredients:

- **Whole Wheat Bread:** 4 slices
- **Ricotta Cheese:** 1/2 cup, low-fat
- **Mixed Berries:** 1 cup (e.g., blueberries, strawberries, raspberries)
- **Egg Whites:** 4 large (or 1/2 cup liquid egg whites)
- **Unsweetened Almond Milk:** 1/2 cup
- **Vanilla Extract:** 1 tsp
- **Cinnamon:** 1/2 tsp
- **Olive Oil Spray:** For cooking
- **Maple Syrup:** 1 tbsp (optional)

Nutritional Information (Per Serving):
- Calories: 320
- Protein: 14g
- Carbohydrates: 40g
- Fats: 10g
- Fiber: 8g
- Cholesterol: 10mg
- Sodium: 350mg
- Potassium: 400mg

Instructions:

1. **Prepare the Ricotta Filling:**
   - In a small bowl, mix ricotta cheese with half of the mixed berries.
2. **Stuff the Bread:**
   - Spread the ricotta and berry mixture on two slices of bread.
   - Top with the remaining two slices to make sandwiches.
3. **Prepare the Egg Mixture:**
   - In a shallow bowl, whisk together egg whites, almond milk, vanilla extract, and cinnamon.
4. **Cook the French Toast:**
   - Preheat a non-stick skillet over medium heat and lightly coat with olive oil spray.
   - Dip each sandwich into the egg mixture, ensuring both sides are well coated.
   - Cook in the skillet for 3-4 minutes on each side, or until golden brown and cooked through.
5. **Serve:**
   - Cut the French toast sandwiches in half.
   - Top with the remaining mixed berries.
   - Drizzle with maple syrup if using and serve immediately.

CHAPTER 2. SNACKS AND APPETIZERS

1. Spicy Hummus and Veggie Sticks

Yield: 4 servings   *Prepration time:* 10 Minutes   *Cooking Time:* 0 Minutes

Nutritional Information (Per Serving):
- **Calories:** 200
- **Protein:** 6g
- **Carbohydrates:** 22g
- **Fats:** 10g
- **Fiber:** 6g
- **Cholesterol:** 0mg
- **Sodium:** 320mg
- **Potassium:** 400mg

Ingredients:

- **Chickpeas:** 1 can (15 oz), drained and rinsed
- **Tahini:** 1/4 cup
- **Lemon Juice:** 2 tbsp
- **Olive Oil:** 2 tbsp
- **Garlic:** 1 clove
- **Ground Cumin:** 1 tsp
- **Paprika:** 1/2 tsp
- **Cayenne Pepper:** 1/4 tsp (adjust to taste)
- **Salt:** 1/2 tsp
- **Water:** 2-3 tbsp (for desired consistency)
- **Carrots:** 2, cut into sticks
- **Celery Sticks:** 2, cut into sticks
- **Bell Pepper:** 1, cut into sticks
- **Cucumber:** 1, cut into sticks

Customizable Ingredients or Garnishes:
- **Cherry Tomatoes:** 1 cup
- **Radishes:** 1 cup, sliced
- **Broccoli Florets:** 1 cup
- **Cauliflower Florets:** 1 cup

Instructions:

1. **Prepare the Hummus:**
   - In a food processor, combine chickpeas, tahini, lemon juice, olive oil, garlic, cumin, paprika, cayenne pepper, and salt.
   - Blend until smooth, adding water as needed to reach desired consistency.
2. **Serve:**
   - Transfer the hummus to a serving bowl.
   - Arrange the veggie sticks around the hummus.
   - Add any additional veggies or garnishes as desired.

2. Baked Kale Chips

🍽 Yield: 4 servings   ✂ Prepration time: 10 Minutes   ⏲ Cooking Time: 20 Minutes

Ingredients:

- **Kale:** 1 bunch, washed and dried
- **Olive Oil:** 1 tbsp
- **Salt:** 1/4 tsp
- **Paprika:** 1/2 tsp (optional)

Customizable Ingredients or Garnishes:
- **Garlic Powder:** 1/4 tsp
- **Nutritional Yeast:** 2 tbsp (for a cheesy flavor)
- **Cayenne Pepper:** 1/4 tsp (for a spicy kick)

Nutritional Information (Per Serving):
- **Calories:** 60
- **Protein:** 3g
- **Carbohydrates:** 6g
- **Fats:** 3g
- **Fiber:** 2g
- **Cholesterol:** 0mg
- **Sodium:** 150mg
- **Potassium:** 350mg

Instructions:

1. **Preheat the Oven:**
   - Preheat the oven to 300°F (150°C).
2. **Prepare the Kale:**
   - Remove the kale leaves from the stems and tear into bite-sized pieces.
   - In a large bowl, toss the kale with olive oil, salt, and paprika (if using).
3. **Bake the Kale Chips:**
   - Spread the kale in a single layer on a baking sheet.
   - Bake for 20 minutes, turning halfway through, until crisp.
4. **Serve:**
   - Allow the kale chips to cool slightly before serving.
   - Add any additional seasonings or garnishes as desired.

3. Quinoa-Stuffed Mini Bell Peppers

Yield: 4 servings   Prepration time: 15 Minutes   Cooking Time: 20 Minutes

Ingredients:

- **Mini Bell Peppers:** 12
- **Quinoa:** 1/2 cup, uncooked
- **Water:** 1 cup
- **Black Beans:** 1/2 cup, cooked
- **Corn:** 1/2 cup, cooked
- **Tomato:** 1, diced
- **Red Onion:** 1/4 cup, finely chopped
- **Cilantro:** 2 tbsp, chopped
- **Lime Juice:** 1 tbsp
- **Olive Oil:** 1 tbsp
- **Salt:** 1/2 tsp
- **Black Pepper:** 1/4 tsp

Nutritional Information (Per Serving):
- **Calories:** 180
- **Protein:** 5g
- **Carbohydrates:** 28g
- **Fats:** 5g
- **Fiber:** 6g
- **Cholesterol:** 0mg
- **Sodium:** 250mg
- **Potassium:** 500mg

Customizable Ingredients or Garnishes:
- **Avocado:** 1, diced
- **Hot Sauce:** To taste
- **Feta Cheese:** 1/4 cup, crumbled (optional)
- **Green Onions:** 2 tbsp, chopped

Instructions:

1. **Cook the Quinoa:**
    - In a medium saucepan, bring water to a boil.
    - Add quinoa, reduce heat, cover, and simmer for 15 minutes until water is absorbed.
2. **Prepare the Bell Peppers:**
    - Preheat the oven to 375°F (190°C).
    - Cut the tops off the mini bell peppers and remove the seeds.
3. **Make the Filling:**
    - In a large bowl, combine cooked quinoa, black beans, corn, tomato, red onion, cilantro, lime juice, olive oil, salt, and black pepper.
4. **Stuff the Peppers:**
    - Spoon the quinoa mixture into each bell pepper.
5. **Bake the Peppers:**
    - Arrange the stuffed peppers on a baking sheet.
    - Bake for 20 minutes, or until the peppers are tender.
6. **Serve:**
    - Serve immediately, adding any customizable ingredients or garnishes as desired.

4. Cucumber and Dill Greek Yogurt Dip

Yield: 4 servings | Prepration time: 10 Minutes | Cooking Time: 0 Minutes

Nutritional Information (Per Serving):
- Calories: 70
- Protein: 7g
- Carbohydrates: 6g
- Fats: 2g
- Fiber: 1g
- Cholesterol: 5mg
- Sodium: 150mg
- Potassium: 200mg

Ingredients:

- **Greek Yogurt:** 1 cup, low-fat
- **Cucumber:** 1/2, grated and drained
- **Garlic:** 1 clove, minced
- **Fresh Dill:** 2 tbsp, chopped
- **Lemon Juice:** 1 tbsp
- **Salt:** 1/4 tsp
- **Black Pepper:** 1/4 tsp

Customizable Ingredients or Garnishes:
- **Red Pepper Flakes:** 1/4 tsp (for a spicy kick)
- **Chopped Mint:** 1 tbsp
- **Olive Oil:** 1 tsp (drizzle on top)
- **Chopped Scallions:** 2 tbsp

Instructions:

1. **Prepare the Cucumber:**
   - Grate the cucumber and squeeze out excess moisture using a cheesecloth or paper towel.
2. **Make the Dip:**
   - In a bowl, combine Greek yogurt, grated cucumber, garlic, fresh dill, lemon juice, salt, and black pepper.
   - Mix well to combine.
3. **Serve:**
   - Transfer to a serving bowl.
   - Add any additional seasonings or garnishes as desired.

5. Sweet Potato and Black Bean Bites

Yield: 4 servings Prepration time: 15 Minutes Cooking Time: 25 Minutes

Nutritional Information (Per Serving):
- Calories: 180
- Protein: 5g
- Carbohydrates: 30g
- Fats: 5g
- Fiber: 7g
- Cholesterol: 0mg
- Sodium: 250mg
- Potassium: 450mg

Ingredients:

- **Sweet Potatoes:** 2, peeled and grated
- **Black Beans:** 1 cup, cooked and mashed
- **Corn:** 1/2 cup, cooked
- **Red Onion:** 1/4 cup, finely chopped
- **Cilantro:** 2 tbsp, chopped
- **Cumin:** 1 tsp
- **Chili Powder:** 1/2 tsp
- **Salt:** 1/2 tsp
- **Olive Oil:** 2 tbsp

Customizable Ingredients or Garnishes:
- **Avocado:** 1, sliced
- **Sour Cream or Greek Yogurt:** 1/4 cup, low-fat
- **Salsa:** 1/2 cup
- **Lime Wedges:** For serving

Instructions:

1. **Preheat the Oven:**
   - Preheat the oven to 400°F (200°C).
2. **Prepare the Mixture:**
   - In a large bowl, combine grated sweet potatoes, mashed black beans, corn, red onion, cilantro, cumin, chili powder, and salt.
   - Mix well to combine.
3. **Form the Bites:**
   - Using your hands, form the mixture into small patties or balls.
4. **Bake the Bites:**
   - Place the bites on a baking sheet lined with parchment paper.
   - Brush with olive oil.
   - Bake for 25 minutes, turning halfway through, until golden brown and crispy.
5. **Serve:**
   - Serve immediately with customizable ingredients or garnishes as desired.

6. Almond-Crusted Zucchini Fries

Yield: 4 servings Prepration time: 15 Minutes Cooking Time: 20 Minutes

Ingredients:

- **Zucchini:** 2 medium, cut into fries
- **Almond Flour:** 1 cup
- **Egg Whites:** 2 large (or 1/4 cup liquid egg whites)
- **Garlic Powder:** 1 tsp
- **Paprika:** 1 tsp
- **Salt:** 1/2 tsp
- **Black Pepper:** 1/4 tsp
- **Olive Oil Spray:** For cooking

Customizable Ingredients or Garnishes:
- **Parmesan Cheese:** 1/4 cup, grated (optional)
- **Fresh Parsley:** 2 tbsp, chopped
- **Marinara Sauce:** 1/2 cup, for dipping
- **Greek Yogurt:** 1/2 cup, for dipping

Nutritional Information (Per Serving):
- **Calories:** 180
- **Protein:** 6g
- **Carbohydrates:** 10g
- **Fats:** 12g
- **Fiber:** 4g
- **Cholesterol:** 0mg
- **Sodium:** 320mg
- **Potassium:** 350mg

Instructions:

1. **Preheat the Oven:**
   - Preheat the oven to 425°F (220°C).
   - Line a baking sheet with parchment paper and spray with olive oil.
2. **Prepare the Breading:**
   - In a shallow bowl, mix almond flour, garlic powder, paprika, salt, and black pepper.
3. **Coat the Zucchini:**
   - Dip each zucchini fry in the egg whites, then coat with the almond flour mixture.
   - Place the coated zucchini fries on the prepared baking sheet.
4. **Bake the Fries:**
   - Lightly spray the zucchini fries with olive oil.
   - Bake for 20 minutes, turning halfway through, until golden brown and crispy.
5. **Serve:**
   - Garnish with optional Parmesan cheese and fresh parsley if desired.
   - Serve immediately with marinara sauce or Greek yogurt for dipping.

7. Roasted Red Pepper and Walnut Dip

Yield: 4 servings Prepration time: 10 Minutes Cooking Time: 0 Minutes

Nutritional Information (Per Serving):
- Calories: 150
- Protein: 3g
- Carbohydrates: 6g
- Fats: 14g
- Fiber: 3g
- Cholesterol: 0mg
- Sodium: 300mg
- Potassium: 250mg

Ingredients:

- **Roasted Red Peppers:** 2 large, from a jar or homemade
- **Walnuts:** 1/2 cup
- **Olive Oil:** 2 tbsp
- **Garlic:** 1 clove
- **Lemon Juice:** 1 tbsp
- **Ground Cumin:** 1 tsp
- **Salt:** 1/2 tsp
- **Black Pepper:** 1/4 tsp

Customizable Ingredients or Garnishes:
- **Paprika:** 1/2 tsp (for garnish)
- **Fresh Parsley:** 2 tbsp, chopped
- **Whole Wheat Pita Chips:** For serving
- **Vegetable Sticks:** For serving (carrots, celery, cucumber)

Instructions:

1. **Prepare the Dip:**
   - In a food processor, combine roasted red peppers, walnuts, olive oil, garlic, lemon juice, cumin, salt, and black pepper.
   - Blend until smooth.
2. **Serve:**
   - Transfer to a serving bowl.
   - Garnish with paprika and fresh parsley if desired.
   - Serve with whole wheat pita chips or vegetable sticks.

8. Low-Fat Spinach Artichoke Dip

Yield: 4 servings Prepration time: 10 Minutes Cooking Time: 15 Minutes

Nutritional Information (Per Serving):
- Calories: 120
- Protein: 8g
- Carbohydrates: 10g
- Fats: 6g
- Fiber: 3g
- Cholesterol: 15mg
- Sodium: 400mg
- Potassium: 350mg

Ingredients:

- **Spinach:** 2 cups, fresh, chopped
- **Artichoke Hearts:** 1 can (14 oz), drained and chopped
- **Low-Fat Greek Yogurt:** 1 cup
- **Low-Fat Cream Cheese:** 1/2 cup
- **Parmesan Cheese:** 1/4 cup, grated
- **Garlic Powder:** 1 tsp
- **Onion Powder:** 1/2 tsp
- **Salt:** 1/2 tsp
- **Black Pepper:** 1/4 tsp

Customizable Ingredients or Garnishes:
- **Red Pepper Flakes:** 1/4 tsp (for a spicy kick)
- **Fresh Dill:** 1 tbsp, chopped
- **Whole Wheat Crackers:** For serving
- **Vegetable Sticks:** For serving (bell peppers, carrots, celery)

Instructions:

1. **Preheat the Oven:**
   - Preheat the oven to 375°F (190°C).
2. **Prepare the Dip:**
   - In a medium bowl, mix together Greek yogurt, cream cheese, Parmesan cheese, garlic powder, onion powder, salt, and black pepper.
   - Fold in chopped spinach and artichoke hearts.
3. **Bake the Dip:**
   - Transfer the mixture to a baking dish.
   - Bake for 15 minutes, or until the dip is bubbly and lightly browned on top.
4. **Serve:**
   - Garnish with red pepper flakes and fresh dill if desired.
   - Serve with whole wheat crackers or vegetable sticks.

9. Edamame and Sea Salt

Yield: 4 servings   Prepration time: 5 Minutes   Cooking Time: 5 Minutes

Ingredients:

- **Edamame:** 2 cups, in pods
- **Sea Salt:** 1/2 tsp

Customizable Ingredients or Garnishes:
- **Red Pepper Flakes:** 1/4 tsp (for a spicy kick)
- **Lemon Zest:** 1 tsp (for a citrusy flavor)
- **Garlic Powder:** 1/4 tsp

Nutritional Information (Per Serving):
- **Calories:** 90
- **Protein:** 8g
- **Carbohydrates:** 8g
- **Fats:** 3g
- **Fiber:** 4g
- **Cholesterol:** 0mg
- **Sodium:** 150mg
- **Potassium:** 250mg

Instructions:

1. **Cook the Edamame:**
   - Bring a pot of water to a boil.
   - Add edamame and cook for 5 minutes.
   - Drain and transfer to a serving bowl.
2. **Season the Edamame:**
   - Sprinkle with sea salt.
   - Add any additional seasonings or garnishes as desired.
3. **Serve:**
   - Serve immediately.

10. Avocado and Tomato Bruschetta

Yield: 4 servings Prepration time: 10 Minutes Cooking Time: 0 Minutes

Nutritional Information (Per Serving):
- Calories: 180
- Protein: 5g
- Carbohydrates: 22g
- Fats: 9g
- Fiber: 6g
- Cholesterol: 0mg
- Sodium: 220mg
- Potassium: 450mg

Ingredients:

- **Whole Grain Baguette:** 1 small, sliced and toasted
- **Avocado:** 1, diced
- **Cherry Tomatoes:** 1 cup, quartered
- **Red Onion:** 1/4 cup, finely chopped
- **Basil:** 2 tbsp, chopped
- **Olive Oil:** 1 tbsp
- **Lemon Juice:** 1 tbsp
- **Salt:** 1/4 tsp
- **Black Pepper:** 1/4 tsp

Customizable Ingredients or Garnishes:
- **Balsamic Glaze:** For drizzling
- **Feta Cheese:** 1/4 cup, crumbled (optional)
- **Garlic:** 1 clove, minced (for extra flavor)

Instructions:

1. **Prepare the Topping:**
   - In a medium bowl, combine diced avocado, cherry tomatoes, red onion, basil, olive oil, lemon juice, salt, and black pepper.
   - Mix gently to combine.
2. **Assemble the Bruschetta:**
   - Spoon the avocado and tomato mixture onto the toasted baguette slices.
3. **Serve:**
   - Drizzle with balsamic glaze if desired.
   - Add crumbled feta cheese or minced garlic for extra flavor if using.
   - Serve immediately.

CHAPTER 3. FISH AND SEAFOOD

1. Grilled Lemon Herb Salmon

Yield: 4 servings Prepration time: 10 Minutes Cooking Time: 15 Minutes

Nutritional Information (Per Serving):
- Calories: 300
- Protein: 34g
- Carbohydrates: 2g
- Fats: 18g
- Fiber: 0g
- Cholesterol: 70mg
- Sodium: 250mg
- Potassium: 800mg

Ingredients:

- **Salmon Fillets:** 4 (about 6 oz each)
- **Olive Oil:** 2 tbsp
- **Lemon Juice:** 2 tbsp
- **Garlic:** 2 cloves, minced
- **Fresh Dill:** 2 tbsp, chopped
- **Salt:** 1/2 tsp
- **Black Pepper:** 1/4 tsp
- **Lemon Slices:** For garnish

Customizable Ingredients or Garnishes:
- **Fresh Parsley:** 2 tbsp, chopped
- **Capers:** 1 tbsp
- **Red Pepper Flakes:** 1/4 tsp (for a spicy kick)

Instructions:

1. **Prepare the Marinade:**
   - In a small bowl, whisk together olive oil, lemon juice, minced garlic, fresh dill, salt, and black pepper.
2. **Marinate the Salmon:**
   - Place the salmon fillets in a shallow dish and pour the marinade over them.
   - Let the salmon marinate for at least 15 minutes.
3. **Preheat the Grill:**
   - Preheat the grill to medium-high heat.
4. **Grill the Salmon:**
   - Place the salmon fillets on the grill, skin-side down.
   - Grill for about 6-8 minutes per side, or until the salmon is cooked through and flakes easily with a fork.
5. **Serve:**
   - Garnish with lemon slices, fresh parsley, capers, and red pepper flakes if desired.
   - Serve immediately.

2. Baked Cod with Garlic and Herbs

Yield: 4 servings Prepration time: 10 Minutes Cooking Time: 20 Minutes

Ingredients:

- **Cod Fillets:** 4 (about 6 oz each)
- **Olive Oil:** 2 tbsp
- **Garlic:** 3 cloves, minced
- **Fresh Thyme:** 1 tbsp, chopped
- **Fresh Parsley:** 2 tbsp, chopped
- **Lemon Juice:** 2 tbsp
- **Salt:** 1/2 tsp
- **Black Pepper:** 1/4 tsp

Nutritional Information (Per Serving):
- Calories: 220
- Protein: 32g
- Carbohydrates: 1g
- Fats: 10g
- Fiber: 0g
- Cholesterol: 75mg
- Sodium: 300mg
- Potassium: 700mg

Customizable Ingredients or Garnishes:
- **Lemon Zest:** 1 tsp
- **Capers:** 1 tbsp
- **Red Pepper Flakes:** 1/4 tsp (for a spicy kick)

Instructions:

1. **Preheat the Oven:**
   - Preheat the oven to 400°F (200°C).
   - Line a baking sheet with parchment paper.
2. **Prepare the Herb Mixture:**
   - In a small bowl, mix together olive oil, minced garlic, fresh thyme, fresh parsley, lemon juice, salt, and black pepper.
3. **Bake the Cod:**
   - Place the cod fillets on the prepared baking sheet.
   - Spoon the herb mixture over the fillets, spreading it evenly.
   - Bake for 15-20 minutes, or until the cod is cooked through and flakes easily with a fork.
4. **Serve:**
   - Garnish with lemon zest, capers, and red pepper flakes if desired.
   - Serve immediately.

3. Shrimp and Avocado Salad

Yield: 4 servings *Prepration time: 15 Minutes* *Cooking Time: 5 Minutes*

Nutritional Information (Per Serving):
- **Calories:** 250
- **Protein:** 25g
- **Carbohydrates:** 12g
- **Fats:** 14g
- **Fiber:** 7g
- **Cholesterol:** 180mg
- **Sodium:** 450mg
- **Potassium:** 700mg

Ingredients:

- **Shrimp:** 1 lb, peeled and deveined
- **Olive Oil:** 1 tbsp
- **Garlic Powder:** 1/2 tsp
- **Salt:** 1/2 tsp
- **Black Pepper:** 1/4 tsp
- **Avocado:** 2, diced
- **Cherry Tomatoes:** 1 cup, halved
- **Cucumber:** 1, diced
- **Red Onion:** 1/4 cup, finely chopped
- **Fresh Cilantro:** 1/4 cup, chopped
- **Lime Juice:** 2 tbsp

Customizable Ingredients or Garnishes:
- **Feta Cheese:** 1/4 cup, crumbled (optional)
- **Jalapeño:** 1, finely chopped (for a spicy kick)
- **Mixed Greens:** 4 cups (for serving)

Instructions:

1. **Cook the Shrimp:**
   - In a skillet, heat olive oil over medium heat.
   - Add shrimp, garlic powder, salt, and black pepper.
   - Cook for 2-3 minutes per side, or until shrimp are pink and opaque.
   - Remove from heat and let cool slightly.
2. **Prepare the Salad:**
   - In a large bowl, combine diced avocado, cherry tomatoes, cucumber, red onion, and fresh cilantro.
3. **Assemble the Salad:**
   - Add the cooked shrimp to the salad.
   - Drizzle with lime juice and toss gently to combine.
4. **Serve:**
   - Garnish with optional feta cheese and jalapeño.
   - Serve over mixed greens if desired.

4. Seared Tuna with Mango Salsa

> Yield: 4 servings   Prepration time: 15 Minutes   Cooking Time: 10 Minutes

Ingredients:

- **Tuna Steaks:** 4 (about 6 oz each)
- **Olive Oil:** 2 tbsp
- **Salt:** 1/2 tsp
- **Black Pepper:** 1/4 tsp

Mango Salsa:
- **Mango:** 1, diced
- **Red Bell Pepper:** 1, diced
- **Red Onion:** 1/4 cup, finely chopped
- **Fresh Cilantro:** 1/4 cup, chopped
- **Lime Juice:** 2 tbsp
- **Salt:** 1/4 tsp
- **Jalapeño:** 1, finely chopped (optional)

Nutritional Information (Per Serving):
- **Calories:** 300
- **Protein:** 38g
- **Carbohydrates:** 12g
- **Fats:** 12g
- **Fiber:** 3g
- **Cholesterol:** 80mg
- **Sodium:** 400mg
- **Potassium:** 800mg

Customizable Ingredients or Garnishes:
- **Avocado:** 1, diced
- **Cucumber:** 1, diced
- **Mixed Greens:** 4 cups (for serving)

Instructions:

1. **Prepare the Mango Salsa:**
   - In a bowl, combine diced mango, red bell pepper, red onion, fresh cilantro, lime juice, salt, and optional jalapeño.
   - Mix well and set aside.
2. **Season the Tuna:**
   - Rub the tuna steaks with olive oil, salt, and black pepper.
3. **Sear the Tuna:**
   - Heat a skillet over medium-high heat.
   - Sear the tuna steaks for 2-3 minutes per side, or until desired doneness is reached.
   - Remove from heat and let rest for a few minutes.
4. **Serve:**
   - Top each tuna steak with a generous spoonful of mango salsa.
   - Serve with optional diced avocado, cucumber, and mixed greens.

5. Spicy Fish Tacos with Cabbage Slaw

Yield: 4 servings (2 tacos per serving) *Prepration time: 15 Minutes* *Cooking Time: 10 Minutes*

Ingredients:

- **White Fish Fillets:** 1 lb (e.g., tilapia, cod)
- **Olive Oil:** 1 tbsp
- **Chili Powder:** 1 tsp
- **Cumin:** 1/2 tsp
- **Garlic Powder:** 1/2 tsp
- **Salt:** 1/2 tsp
- **Black Pepper:** 1/4 tsp
- **Corn Tortillas:** 8

Cabbage Slaw:
- **Green Cabbage:** 2 cups, shredded
- **Red Cabbage:** 1 cup, shredded
- **Carrot:** 1, grated
- **Cilantro:** 1/4 cup, chopped
- **Lime Juice:** 2 tbsp
- **Olive Oil:** 1 tbsp
- **Salt:** 1/4 tsp
- **Black Pepper:** 1/4 tsp

Nutritional Information (Per Serving):
- **Calories:** 280
- **Protein:** 24g
- **Carbohydrates:** 24g
- **Fats:** 12g
- **Fiber:** 6g
- **Cholesterol:** 55mg
- **Sodium:** 400mg
- **Potassium:** 700mg

Customizable Ingredients or Garnishes:
- **Avocado:** 1, sliced
- **Salsa:** 1/2 cup
- **Greek Yogurt:** 1/4 cup (for a creamy topping)
- **Jalapeño:** 1, sliced (for a spicy kick)

Instructions:

1. **Prepare the Cabbage Slaw:**
   - In a large bowl, combine shredded green cabbage, red cabbage, grated carrot, chopped cilantro, lime juice, olive oil, salt, and black pepper.
   - Toss to combine and set aside.
2. **Season the Fish:**
   - In a small bowl, mix chili powder, cumin, garlic powder, salt, and black pepper.
   - Rub the fish fillets with olive oil and the spice mixture.
3. **Cook the Fish:**
   - Heat a skillet over medium-high heat.
   - Cook the fish fillets for 3-4 minutes per side, or until the fish is cooked through and flakes easily with a fork.
   - Remove from heat and flake the fish into pieces.
4. **Assemble the Tacos:**
   - Warm the corn tortillas.
   - Divide the fish evenly among the tortillas.
   - Top with cabbage slaw and any additional toppings such as avocado slices, salsa, Greek yogurt, or sliced jalapeño.
5. **Serve:**
   - Serve immediately.

6. Steamed Mussels in White Wine Sauce

Yield: 4 servings Prepration time: 10 Minutes Cooking Time: 15 Minutes

Ingredients:

- **Mussels:** 2 lbs, cleaned and debearded
- **Olive Oil:** 2 tbsp
- **Garlic:** 4 cloves, minced
- **Shallots:** 2, finely chopped
- **White Wine:** 1 cup, dry
- **Lemon Juice:** 2 tbsp
- **Fresh Parsley:** 1/4 cup, chopped
- **Salt:** 1/2 tsp
- **Black Pepper:** 1/4 tsp

Customizable Ingredients or Garnishes:
- **Red Pepper Flakes:** 1/4 tsp (for a spicy kick)
- **Fresh Thyme:** 1 tbsp, chopped
- **Whole Grain Bread:** For serving

Nutritional Information (Per Serving):
- **Calories:** 250
- **Protein:** 24g
- **Carbohydrates:** 6g
- **Fats:** 10g
- **Fiber:** 0g
- **Cholesterol:** 50mg
- **Sodium:** 550mg
- **Potassium:** 500mg

Instructions:

1. **Prepare the Sauce:**
   - In a large pot, heat olive oil over medium heat.
   - Add minced garlic and shallots and sauté until fragrant, about 2 minutes.
2. **Add Wine and Mussels:**
   - Pour in the white wine and lemon juice, and bring to a simmer.
   - Add the mussels, cover the pot, and steam for 5-7 minutes, or until the mussels open.
3. **Finish the Dish:**
   - Discard any mussels that do not open.
   - Stir in fresh parsley, salt, and black pepper.
4. **Serve:**
   - Serve immediately with optional red pepper flakes and fresh thyme for garnish.
   - Enjoy with whole grain bread if desired.

7. Coconut Crusted Tilapia

🍽 Yield: 4 servings ⏲ Prepration time: 15 Minutes 👨‍🍳 Cooking Time: 20 Minutes

Nutritional Information (Per Serving):
- Calories: 320
- Protein: 28g
- Carbohydrates: 18g
- Fats: 15g
- Fiber: 4g
- Cholesterol: 55mg
- Sodium: 300mg
- Potassium: 600mg

Ingredients:

- **Tilapia Fillets:** 4 (about 6 oz each)
- **Egg Whites:** 2 large
- **Unsweetened Shredded Coconut:** 1 cup
- **Panko Breadcrumbs:** 1/2 cup
- **Salt:** 1/2 tsp
- **Black Pepper:** 1/4 tsp
- **Olive Oil Spray:** For cooking

Customizable Ingredients or Garnishes:
- **Lime Zest:** 1 tsp
- **Fresh Cilantro:** 2 tbsp, chopped
- **Mango Salsa:** 1 cup (for serving)

Instructions:

1. **Preheat the Oven:**
   - Preheat the oven to 375°F (190°C).
   - Line a baking sheet with parchment paper and spray with olive oil.
2. **Prepare the Coating:**
   - In a shallow bowl, whisk egg whites until frothy.
   - In another shallow bowl, combine shredded coconut, panko breadcrumbs, salt, and black pepper.
3. **Coat the Tilapia:**
   - Dip each tilapia fillet into the egg whites, then coat with the coconut mixture.
   - Place the coated fillets on the prepared baking sheet.
4. **Bake the Tilapia:**
   - Spray the tops of the fillets with olive oil.
   - Bake for 15-20 minutes, or until the fish is cooked through and the coating is golden brown.
5. **Serve:**
   - Garnish with lime zest and fresh cilantro if desired.
   - Serve immediately with mango salsa.

8. Garlic Shrimp and Asparagus Stir-Fry

Yield: 4 servings   Prepration time: 10 Minutes   Cooking Time: 10 Minutes

Ingredients:

- **Shrimp:** 1 lb, peeled and deveined
- **Asparagus:** 1 bunch, trimmed and cut into 2-inch pieces
- **Olive Oil:** 2 tbsp
- **Garlic:** 4 cloves, minced
- **Soy Sauce:** 2 tbsp, low-sodium
- **Lemon Juice:** 2 tbsp
- **Red Pepper Flakes:** 1/4 tsp (optional)
- **Salt:** 1/4 tsp
- **Black Pepper:** 1/4 tsp

Customizable Ingredients or Garnishes:
- **Fresh Ginger:** 1 tbsp, minced
- **Sesame Seeds:** 1 tbsp (for garnish)
- **Brown Rice:** 2 cups, cooked (for serving)

Nutritional Information (Per Serving):
- Calories: 180
- Protein: 24g
- Carbohydrates: 5g
- Fats: 7g
- Fiber: 2g
- Cholesterol: 170mg
- Sodium: 470mg
- Potassium: 450mg

Instructions:

1. **Cook the Asparagus:**
   - In a large skillet, heat 1 tbsp of olive oil over medium-high heat.
   - Add the asparagus and cook for 3-4 minutes, until tender-crisp. Remove and set aside.
2. **Cook the Shrimp:**
   - In the same skillet, heat the remaining 1 tbsp of olive oil.
   - Add garlic and cook for 30 seconds.
   - Add shrimp and cook for 2-3 minutes per side, until pink and opaque.
3. **Combine and Season:**
   - Return the asparagus to the skillet.
   - Add soy sauce, lemon juice, red pepper flakes (if using), salt, and black pepper.
   - Stir well to combine and heat through.
4. **Serve:**
   - Garnish with optional fresh ginger and sesame seeds.
   - Serve immediately with cooked brown rice if desired.

9. Mediterranean Baked Halibut

Yield: 4 servings | *Prepration time: 10 Minutes* | *Cooking Time: 25 Minutes*

Nutritional Information (Per Serving):
- Calories: 300
- Protein: 34g
- Carbohydrates: 6g
- Fats: 15g
- Fiber: 2g
- Cholesterol: 70mg
- Sodium: 450mg
- Potassium: 800mg

Ingredients:

- **Halibut Fillets:** 4 (about 6 oz each)
- **Olive Oil:** 2 tbsp
- **Garlic:** 3 cloves, minced
- **Cherry Tomatoes:** 1 cup, halved
- **Kalamata Olives:** 1/4 cup, pitted and sliced
- **Red Onion:** 1/2, thinly sliced
- **Fresh Parsley:** 1/4 cup, chopped
- **Lemon Juice:** 2 tbsp
- **Salt:** 1/2 tsp
- **Black Pepper:** 1/4 tsp

Customizable Ingredients or Garnishes:
- **Feta Cheese:** 1/4 cup, crumbled (optional)
- **Capers:** 2 tbsp
- **Red Pepper Flakes:** 1/4 tsp (for a spicy kick)

Instructions:

1. **Preheat the Oven:**
   - Preheat the oven to 375°F (190°C).
   - Line a baking dish with parchment paper.
2. **Prepare the Topping:**
   - In a bowl, mix together olive oil, minced garlic, cherry tomatoes, Kalamata olives, red onion, fresh parsley, lemon juice, salt, and black pepper.
3. **Bake the Halibut:**
   - Place the halibut fillets in the prepared baking dish.
   - Spoon the tomato and olive mixture over the fillets.
   - Bake for 20-25 minutes, or until the fish is cooked through and flakes easily with a fork.
4. **Serve:**
   - Garnish with optional feta cheese, capers, and red pepper flakes.
   - Serve immediately.

10. Salmon and Quinoa Patties

Yield: 4 servings (8 patties)   *Prepration time: 10 Minutes*   *Cooking Time: 10 Minutes*

Ingredients:

- **Salmon Fillets:** 1 lb, cooked and flaked
- **Quinoa:** 1 cup, cooked
- **Egg Whites:** 2 large
- **Panko Breadcrumbs:** 1/2 cup
- **Green Onion:** 1/4 cup, finely chopped
- **Fresh Dill:** 2 tbsp, chopped
- **Lemon Zest:** 1 tsp
- **Salt:** 1/2 tsp
- **Black Pepper:** 1/4 tsp
- **Olive Oil:** 2 tbsp (for frying)

Customizable Ingredients or Garnishes:
- **Greek Yogurt:** 1/4 cup (for a creamy topping)
- **Avocado:** 1, sliced (for serving)
- **Mixed Greens:** 4 cups (for serving)

Nutritional Information (Per Serving):
- **Calories:** 350
- **Protein:** 28g
- **Carbohydrates:** 20g
- **Fats:** 15g
- **Fiber:** 3g
- **Cholesterol:** 60mg
- **Sodium:** 400mg
- **Potassium:** 700mg

Instructions:

1. **Prepare the Patty Mixture:**
   - In a large bowl, combine flaked salmon, cooked quinoa, egg whites, panko breadcrumbs, green onion, fresh dill, lemon zest, salt, and black pepper.
   - Mix well to combine.
2. **Form the Patties:**
   - Shape the mixture into 8 patties.
3. **Cook the Patties:**
   - Heat olive oil in a large skillet over medium heat.
   - Cook the patties for 3-4 minutes per side, or until golden brown and cooked through.
4. **Serve:**
   - Serve immediately with optional Greek yogurt, avocado slices, and mixed greens.

11. Lemon Dill Baked Salmon

🍲 Yield: 4 servings   🥄 Prepration time: 10 Minutes   👨‍🍳 Cooking Time: 20 Minutes

Nutritional Information (Per Serving):
- Calories: 300
- Protein: 34g
- Carbohydrates: 2g
- Fats: 18g
- Fiber: 0g
- Cholesterol: 70mg
- Sodium: 250mg
- Potassium: 800mg

Ingredients:

- **Salmon Fillets:** 4 (about 6 oz each)
- **Olive Oil:** 2 tbsp
- **Lemon Juice:** 2 tbsp
- **Garlic:** 2 cloves, minced
- **Fresh Dill:** 2 tbsp, chopped
- **Salt:** 1/2 tsp
- **Black Pepper:** 1/4 tsp
- **Lemon Slices:** For garnish

Customizable Ingredients or Garnishes:
- **Capers:** 1 tbsp
- **Fresh Parsley:** 2 tbsp, chopped
- **Red Pepper Flakes:** 1/4 tsp (for a spicy kick)

Instructions:

1. **Preheat the Oven:**
   - Preheat the oven to 375°F (190°C).
   - Line a baking sheet with parchment paper.
2. **Prepare the Marinade:**
   - In a small bowl, whisk together olive oil, lemon juice, minced garlic, fresh dill, salt, and black pepper.
3. **Marinate the Salmon:**
   - Place the salmon fillets on the prepared baking sheet.
   - Brush the marinade over the salmon fillets.
4. **Bake the Salmon:**
   - Bake for 15-20 minutes, or until the salmon is cooked through and flakes easily with a fork.
5. **Serve:**
   - Garnish with lemon slices, capers, fresh parsley, and red pepper flakes if desired.
   - Serve immediately.

12. Shrimp and Vegetable Skewers

Yield: 4 servings | Prepration time: 15 Minutes | Cooking Time: 10 Minutes

Nutritional Information (Per Serving):
- Calories: 180
- Protein: 24g
- Carbohydrates: 8g
- Fats: 7g
- Fiber: 2g
- Cholesterol: 170mg
- Sodium: 400mg
- Potassium: 500mg

Ingredients:

- **Shrimp:** 1 lb, peeled and deveined
- **Red Bell Pepper:** 1, cut into chunks
- **Yellow Bell Pepper:** 1, cut into chunks
- **Red Onion:** 1, cut into chunks
- **Zucchini:** 1, sliced
- **Olive Oil:** 2 tbsp
- **Garlic Powder:** 1/2 tsp
- **Paprika:** 1/2 tsp
- **Salt:** 1/2 tsp
- **Black Pepper:** 1/4 tsp
- **Lemon Juice:** 2 tbsp

Customizable Ingredients or Garnishes:
- **Fresh Basil:** 2 tbsp, chopped
- **Lime Wedges:** For serving
- **Red Pepper Flakes:** 1/4 tsp (for a spicy kick)

Instructions:

1. **Preheat the Grill:**
   - Preheat the grill to medium-high heat.
2. **Prepare the Skewers:**
   - In a large bowl, combine olive oil, garlic powder, paprika, salt, black pepper, and lemon juice.
   - Add shrimp and vegetables to the bowl and toss to coat.
3. **Assemble the Skewers:**
   - Thread the shrimp and vegetables onto skewers.
4. **Grill the Skewers:**
   - Grill the skewers for 2-3 minutes per side, or until the shrimp are pink and opaque, and the vegetables are tender.
5. **Serve:**
   - Garnish with fresh basil and serve with lime wedges and optional red pepper flakes.

13. Parchment-Baked Cod with Vegetables

Yield: 4 servings Prepration time: 15 Minutes Cooking Time: 20 Minutes

Nutritional Information (Per Serving):
- Calories: 250
- Protein: 32g
- Carbohydrates: 8g
- Fats: 10g
- Fiber: 2g
- Cholesterol: 75mg
- Sodium: 300mg
- Potassium: 700mg

Ingredients:

- **Cod Fillets:** 4 (about 6 oz each)
- **Cherry Tomatoes:** 1 cup, halved
- **Zucchini:** 1, sliced
- **Red Bell Pepper:** 1, sliced
- **Red Onion:** 1/2, thinly sliced
- **Olive Oil:** 2 tbsp
- **Lemon Juice:** 2 tbsp
- **Garlic:** 2 cloves, minced
- **Fresh Thyme:** 1 tbsp, chopped
- **Salt:** 1/2 tsp
- **Black Pepper:** 1/4 tsp

Customizable Ingredients or Garnishes:
- **Capers:** 1 tbsp
- **Fresh Basil:** 2 tbsp, chopped
- **Red Pepper Flakes:** 1/4 tsp (for a spicy kick)

Instructions:

1. **Preheat the Oven:**
   - Preheat the oven to 400°F (200°C).
2. **Prepare the Vegetables:**
   - In a bowl, combine cherry tomatoes, zucchini, red bell pepper, and red onion.
   - Toss with olive oil, lemon juice, minced garlic, fresh thyme, salt, and black pepper.
3. **Assemble the Packets:**
   - Cut 4 large pieces of parchment paper.
   - Place one cod fillet in the center of each piece of parchment paper.
   - Divide the vegetable mixture evenly over the cod fillets.
   - Fold the parchment paper to create a sealed packet.
4. **Bake the Cod:**
   - Place the packets on a baking sheet and bake for 15-20 minutes, or until the cod is cooked through and flakes easily with a fork.
5. **Serve:**
   - Garnish with optional capers, fresh basil, and red pepper flakes.
   - Serve immediately.

14. Blackened Mahi Mahi

Yield: 4 servings • *Prepration time: 10 Minutes* • *Cooking Time: 10 Minutes*

Nutritional Information (Per Serving):
- Calories: 220
- Protein: 34g
- Carbohydrates: 2g
- Fats: 8g
- Fiber: 0g
- Cholesterol: 90mg
- Sodium: 400mg
- Potassium: 600mg

Ingredients:

- **Mahi Mahi Fillets:** 4 (about 6 oz each)
- **Olive Oil:** 2 tbsp
- **Paprika:** 1 tsp
- **Garlic Powder:** 1 tsp
- **Onion Powder:** 1 tsp
- **Dried Thyme:** 1/2 tsp
- **Dried Oregano:** 1/2 tsp
- **Cayenne Pepper:** 1/4 tsp
- **Salt:** 1/2 tsp
- **Black Pepper:** 1/4 tsp

Customizable Ingredients or Garnishes:
- **Lemon Wedges:** For serving
- **Fresh Cilantro:** 2 tbsp, chopped
- **Avocado Slices:** For serving

Instructions:

1. **Prepare the Spice Mixture:**
   - In a small bowl, mix together paprika, garlic powder, onion powder, dried thyme, dried oregano, cayenne pepper, salt, and black pepper.
2. **Season the Mahi Mahi:**
   - Rub the spice mixture over both sides of the mahi mahi fillets.
3. **Cook the Mahi Mahi:**
   - Heat olive oil in a skillet over medium-high heat.
   - Cook the fillets for 3-4 minutes per side, or until the fish is cooked through and flakes easily with a fork.
4. **Serve:**
   - Garnish with lemon wedges, fresh cilantro, and avocado slices.
   - Serve immediately.

15. Grilled Shrimp with Pineapple Salsa

Yield: 4 servings   Prepration time: 15 Minutes   Cooking Time: 10 Minutes

Ingredients:

- **Shrimp:** 1 lb, peeled and deveined
- **Olive Oil:** 2 tbsp
- **Garlic Powder:** 1/2 tsp
- **Chili Powder:** 1/2 tsp
- **Salt:** 1/2 tsp
- **Black Pepper:** 1/4 tsp

Pineapple Salsa:
- **Pineapple:** 1 cup, diced
- **Red Bell Pepper:** 1/2, diced
- **Red Onion:** 1/4 cup, finely chopped
- **Fresh Cilantro:** 1/4 cup, chopped
- **Lime Juice:** 2 tbsp
- **Salt:** 1/4 tsp

Nutritional Information (Per Serving):
- Calories: 220
- Protein: 24g
- Carbohydrates: 10g
- Fats: 10g
- Fiber: 2g
- Cholesterol: 170mg
- Sodium: 450mg
- Potassium: 500mg

Customizable Ingredients or Garnishes:
- **Jalapeño:** 1, finely chopped (for a spicy kick)
- **Avocado:** 1, diced
- **Mixed Greens:** 4 cups (for serving)

Instructions:

1. **Prepare the Pineapple Salsa:**
   - In a bowl, combine diced pineapple, red bell pepper, red onion, fresh cilantro, lime juice, and salt.
   - Mix well and set aside.
2. **Preheat the Grill:**
   - Preheat the grill to medium-high heat.
3. **Prepare the Shrimp:**
   - In a bowl, toss the shrimp with olive oil, garlic powder, chili powder, salt, and black pepper.
4. **Grill the Shrimp:**
   - Thread the shrimp onto skewers.
   - Grill for 2-3 minutes per side, or until the shrimp are pink and opaque.
5. **Serve:**
   - Top the grilled shrimp with pineapple salsa.
   - Serve with optional jalapeño, diced avocado, and mixed greens.

CHAPTER 4. MEAT DISHES: POULTRY AND BEEF

1. Grilled Chicken and Vegetable Skewers

Yield: 4 servings Prepration time: 15 Minutes Cooking Time: 10 Minutes

Nutritional Information (Per Serving):
- Calories: 250
- Protein: 30g
- Carbohydrates: 8g
- Fats: 10g
- Fiber: 3g
- Cholesterol: 75mg
- Sodium: 400mg
- Potassium: 600mg

Ingredients:

- **Chicken Breast:** 1 lb, cut into cubes
- **Red Bell Pepper:** 1, cut into chunks
- **Yellow Bell Pepper:** 1, cut into chunks
- **Red Onion:** 1, cut into chunks
- **Zucchini:** 1, sliced
- **Olive Oil:** 2 tbsp
- **Garlic Powder:** 1/2 tsp
- **Paprika:** 1/2 tsp
- **Salt:** 1/2 tsp
- **Black Pepper:** 1/4 tsp
- **Lemon Juice:** 2 tbsp

Customizable Ingredients or Garnishes:
- **Fresh Basil:** 2 tbsp, chopped
- **Lime Wedges:** For serving
- **Red Pepper Flakes:** 1/4 tsp (for a spicy kick)

Instructions:

1. **Prepare the Skewers:**
   - In a large bowl, combine olive oil, garlic powder, paprika, salt, black pepper, and lemon juice.
   - Add chicken and vegetables to the bowl and toss to coat.
2. **Assemble the Skewers:**
   - Thread the chicken and vegetables onto skewers.
3. **Grill the Skewers:**
   - Preheat the grill to medium-high heat.
   - Grill the skewers for 3-4 minutes per side, or until the chicken is cooked through and the vegetables are tender.
4. **Serve:**
   - Garnish with fresh basil and serve with lime wedges and optional red pepper flakes.

2. Turkey and Spinach Meatballs

Yield: 4 servings   Prepration time: 15 Minutes   Cooking Time: 25 Minutes

Ingredients:

- **Ground Turkey:** 1 lb, lean
- **Spinach:** 2 cups, fresh, chopped
- **Whole Wheat Breadcrumbs:** 1/2 cup
- **Parmesan Cheese:** 1/4 cup, grated (optional)
- **Egg:** 1 large
- **Garlic:** 2 cloves, minced
- **Onion:** 1/2 cup, finely chopped
- **Salt:** 1/2 tsp
- **Black Pepper:** 1/4 tsp
- **Olive Oil Spray:** For cooking

Customizable Ingredients or Garnishes:
- **Marinara Sauce:** 1 cup (for serving)
- **Fresh Basil:** 2 tbsp, chopped
- **Red Pepper Flakes:** 1/4 tsp (for a spicy kick)

Nutritional Information (Per Serving):
- **Calories:** 230
- **Protein:** 25g
- **Carbohydrates:** 10g
- **Fats:** 10g
- **Fiber:** 2g
- **Cholesterol:** 85mg
- **Sodium:** 450mg
- **Potassium:** 500mg

Instructions:

1. **Preheat the Oven:**
   - Preheat the oven to 400°F (200°C).
   - Line a baking sheet with parchment paper and spray with olive oil.
2. **Prepare the Meatballs:**
   - In a large bowl, combine ground turkey, chopped spinach, whole wheat breadcrumbs, Parmesan cheese (if using), egg, minced garlic, chopped onion, salt, and black pepper.
   - Mix until well combined.
3. **Form the Meatballs:**
   - Shape the mixture into meatballs, about 1 inch in diameter.
   - Place the meatballs on the prepared baking sheet.
4. **Bake the Meatballs:**
   - Bake for 20-25 minutes, or until the meatballs are cooked through and golden brown.
5. **Serve:**
   - Serve with marinara sauce, garnished with fresh basil and optional red pepper flakes.

3. Lemon Herb Roasted Chicken

Yield: 4 servings *Prepration time: 10 Minutes* *Cooking Time: 50 Minutes*

Nutritional Information (Per Serving):
- **Calories:** 300
- **Protein:** 28g
- **Carbohydrates:** 3g
- **Fats:** 20g
- **Fiber:** 1g
- **Cholesterol:** 100mg
- **Sodium:** 400mg
- **Potassium:** 500mg

Ingredients:

- **Chicken Thighs:** 4, bone-in, skinless
- **Olive Oil:** 2 tbsp
- **Lemon Juice:** 2 tbsp
- **Garlic:** 3 cloves, minced
- **Fresh Rosemary:** 1 tbsp, chopped
- **Fresh Thyme:** 1 tbsp, chopped
- **Salt:** 1/2 tsp
- **Black Pepper:** 1/4 tsp
- **Lemon Slices:** For garnish

Customizable Ingredients or Garnishes:
- **Fresh Parsley:** 2 tbsp, chopped
- **Red Pepper Flakes:** 1/4 tsp (for a spicy kick)

Instructions:

1. **Preheat the Oven:**
   - Preheat the oven to 375°F (190°C).
   - Line a baking dish with parchment paper.
2. **Prepare the Marinade:**
   - In a small bowl, whisk together olive oil, lemon juice, minced garlic, fresh rosemary, fresh thyme, salt, and black pepper.
3. **Marinate the Chicken:**
   - Place the chicken thighs in the baking dish.
   - Pour the marinade over the chicken, making sure it is evenly coated.
4. **Roast the Chicken:**
   - Roast for 45-50 minutes, or until the chicken is cooked through and the juices run clear.
5. **Serve:**
   - Garnish with lemon slices, fresh parsley, and optional red pepper flakes.
   - Serve immediately.

4. Slow-Cooked Beef and Veggie Stew

Yield: 4 servings | *Prepration time: 15 Minutes* | *Cooking Time: 6-8 hours (slow cooker)*

Ingredients:

- **Beef Stew Meat:** 1 lb, lean, cubed
- **Carrots:** 3, sliced
- **Celery:** 3 stalks, sliced
- **Potatoes:** 2, diced
- **Onion:** 1, chopped
- **Garlic:** 3 cloves, minced
- **Tomato Paste:** 2 tbsp
- **Beef Broth:** 4 cups, low-sodium
- **Bay Leaves:** 2
- **Fresh Thyme:** 1 tsp, chopped
- **Salt:** 1/2 tsp
- **Black Pepper:** 1/4 tsp
- **Olive Oil:** 1 tbsp

Customizable Ingredients or Garnishes:
- **Fresh Parsley:** 2 tbsp, chopped
- **Red Pepper Flakes:** 1/4 tsp (for a spicy kick)
- **Whole Grain Bread:** For serving

Nutritional Information (Per Serving):
- Calories: 320
- Protein: 30g
- Carbohydrates: 25g
- Fats: 10g
- Fiber: 5g
- Cholesterol: 75mg
- Sodium: 600mg
- Potassium: 800mg

Instructions:

1. **Prepare the Ingredients:**
   - In a skillet, heat olive oil over medium heat.
   - Add beef stew meat and brown on all sides.
2. **Combine in Slow Cooker:**
   - In a slow cooker, combine browned beef, carrots, celery, potatoes, onion, garlic, tomato paste, beef broth, bay leaves, fresh thyme, salt, and black pepper.
   - Stir well to combine.
3. **Cook the Stew:**
   - Cover and cook on low for 6-8 hours, or until the beef is tender and the vegetables are cooked through.
4. **Serve:**
   - Remove bay leaves before serving.
   - Garnish with fresh parsley and optional red pepper flakes.
   - Serve with whole grain bread if desired.

5. Spicy Turkey Lettuce Wraps

Yield: 4 servings | Prepration time: 10 Minutes | Cooking Time: 15 Minutes

Nutritional Information (Per Serving):
- Calories: 200
- Protein: 22g
- Carbohydrates: 10g
- Fats: 10g
- Fiber: 3g
- Cholesterol: 60mg
- Sodium: 500mg
- Potassium: 500mg

Ingredients:

- **Ground Turkey:** 1 lb, lean
- **Romaine Lettuce Leaves:** 8 large
- **Carrot:** 1, shredded
- **Red Bell Pepper:** 1, diced
- **Garlic:** 2 cloves, minced
- **Ginger:** 1 tbsp, minced
- **Soy Sauce:** 2 tbsp, low-sodium
- **Hoisin Sauce:** 2 tbsp
- **Sriracha Sauce:** 1 tbsp
- **Olive Oil:** 1 tbsp

Customizable Ingredients or Garnishes:
- **Green Onions:** 2 tbsp, sliced
- **Cilantro:** 2 tbsp, chopped
- **Lime Wedges:** For serving

Instructions:

1. **Cook the Turkey:**
   - In a skillet, heat olive oil over medium heat.
   - Add ground turkey and cook until browned, breaking it apart with a spoon.
2. **Add the Vegetables:**
   - Add minced garlic, minced ginger, shredded carrot, and diced red bell pepper to the skillet.
   - Cook for 3-4 minutes, until the vegetables are tender.
3. **Season the Turkey:**
   - Stir in soy sauce, hoisin sauce, and sriracha sauce.
   - Cook for an additional 2 minutes, until the sauce is heated through.
4. **Assemble the Lettuce Wraps:**
   - Spoon the turkey mixture into the center of each romaine lettuce leaf.
5. **Serve:**
   - Garnish with green onions and cilantro.
   - Serve with lime wedges.

6. Chicken and Quinoa Stuffed Peppers

Yield: 4 servings Prepration time: 15 Minutes Cooking Time: 30 Minutes

Ingredients:

- **Bell Peppers:** 4 large, tops cut off and seeds removed
- **Cooked Chicken Breast:** 1 cup, shredded
- **Quinoa:** 1 cup, cooked
- **Black Beans:** 1/2 cup, cooked
- **Corn:** 1/2 cup, cooked
- **Tomato:** 1, diced
- **Onion:** 1/4 cup, finely chopped
- **Cumin:** 1 tsp
- **Chili Powder:** 1 tsp
- **Salt:** 1/2 tsp
- **Black Pepper:** 1/4 tsp
- **Olive Oil:** 1 tbsp
- **Fresh Cilantro:** 2 tbsp, chopped

Nutritional Information (Per Serving):
- Calories: 300
- Protein: 25g
- Carbohydrates: 30g
- Fats: 10g
- Fiber: 8g
- Cholesterol: 50mg
- Sodium: 500mg
- Potassium: 800mg

Customizable Ingredients or Garnishes:
- **Cheddar Cheese:** 1/4 cup, shredded (optional)
- **Avocado:** 1, diced
- **Salsa:** 1/2 cup (for serving)

Instructions:

1. **Preheat the Oven:**
   - Preheat the oven to 375°F (190°C).
2. **Prepare the Filling:**
   - In a large bowl, combine shredded chicken, cooked quinoa, black beans, corn, diced tomato, chopped onion, cumin, chili powder, salt, and black pepper.
   - Mix until well combined.
3. **Stuff the Peppers:**
   - Spoon the filling into the bell peppers.
4. **Bake the Peppers:**
   - Place the stuffed peppers in a baking dish.
   - Drizzle with olive oil.
   - Bake for 25-30 minutes, or until the peppers are tender.
5. **Serve:**
   - Garnish with fresh cilantro and optional cheddar cheese.
   - Serve with diced avocado and salsa.

7. Ginger Beef Stir-Fry

Yield: 4 servings Prepration time: 15 Minutes Cooking Time: 10 Minutes

Ingredients:

- **Beef Sirloin:** 1 lb, thinly sliced
- **Broccoli Florets:** 2 cups
- **Red Bell Pepper:** 1, sliced
- **Carrot:** 1, sliced
- **Garlic:** 2 cloves, minced
- **Ginger:** 1 tbsp, minced
- **Soy Sauce:** 3 tbsp, low-sodium
- **Honey:** 1 tbsp
- **Olive Oil:** 2 tbsp
- **Cornstarch:** 1 tbsp (optional, for thickening)
- **Water:** 1/4 cup

Customizable Ingredients or Garnishes:
- **Sesame Seeds:** 1 tbsp
- **Green Onions:** 2 tbsp, sliced
- **Brown Rice:** 2 cups, cooked (for serving)

Nutritional Information (Per Serving):
- **Calories:** 350
- **Protein:** 30g
- **Carbohydrates:** 20g
- **Fats:** 15g
- **Fiber:** 4g
- **Cholesterol:** 75mg
- **Sodium:** 600mg
- **Potassium:** 700mg

Instructions:

1. **Prepare the Sauce:**
   - In a small bowl, whisk together soy sauce, honey, and water.
   - If using, mix in cornstarch for thickening.
2. **Cook the Beef:**
   - In a large skillet or wok, heat 1 tbsp olive oil over medium-high heat.
   - Add the beef slices and cook for 2-3 minutes until browned.
   - Remove from the skillet and set aside.
3. **Cook the Vegetables:**
   - In the same skillet, heat the remaining 1 tbsp olive oil.
   - Add minced garlic and ginger, and cook for 1 minute until fragrant.
   - Add broccoli, red bell pepper, and carrot, and stir-fry for 3-4 minutes until tender-crisp.
4. **Combine and Serve:**
   - Return the beef to the skillet and pour in the sauce.
   - Stir well to combine and heat through.
5. **Serve:**
   - Garnish with sesame seeds and green onions.
   - Serve with cooked brown rice.

8. BBQ Chicken and Pineapple Kebabs

Yield: 4 servings   Prepration time: 15 Minutes   Cooking Time: 15 Minutes

Ingredients:

- **Chicken Breast:** 1 lb, cut into cubes
- **Pineapple Chunks:** 2 cups (fresh or canned, drained)
- **Red Bell Pepper:** 1, cut into chunks
- **Red Onion:** 1, cut into chunks
- **BBQ Sauce:** 1/2 cup, low-sodium
- **Olive Oil:** 1 tbsp
- **Salt:** 1/2 tsp
- **Black Pepper:** 1/4 tsp

Customizable Ingredients or Garnishes:
- **Fresh Cilantro:** 2 tbsp, chopped
- **Lime Wedges:** For serving
- **Red Pepper Flakes:** 1/4 tsp (for a spicy kick)

Nutritional Information (Per Serving):
- **Calories:** 280
- **Protein:** 25g
- **Carbohydrates:** 20g
- **Fats:** 10g
- **Fiber:** 3g
- **Cholesterol:** 75mg
- **Sodium:** 450mg
- **Potassium:** 500mg

Instructions:

1. **Prepare the Skewers:**
   - In a large bowl, combine chicken, pineapple, red bell pepper, and red onion.
   - Drizzle with olive oil, and season with salt and black pepper.
   - Toss to coat evenly.
2. **Assemble the Skewers:**
   - Thread the chicken, pineapple, and vegetables onto skewers, alternating pieces.
3. **Grill the Skewers:**
   - Preheat the grill to medium-high heat.
   - Grill the skewers for 10-12 minutes, turning occasionally and basting with BBQ sauce during the last 5 minutes of cooking.
4. **Serve:**
   - Garnish with fresh cilantro and serve with lime wedges and optional red pepper flakes.

9. Lemon Garlic Chicken Breasts

Yield: 4 servings   Prepration time: 10 Minutes   Cooking Time: 25 Minutes

Nutritional Information (Per Serving):
- **Calories:** 250
- **Protein:** 30g
- **Carbohydrates:** 3g
- **Fats:** 12g
- **Fiber:** 0g
- **Cholesterol:** 75mg
- **Sodium:** 400mg
- **Potassium:** 500mg

Ingredients:

- **Chicken Breasts:** 4 (about 6 oz each)
- **Olive Oil:** 2 tbsp
- **Lemon Juice:** 2 tbsp
- **Garlic:** 4 cloves, minced
- **Fresh Thyme:** 1 tbsp, chopped
- **Salt:** 1/2 tsp
- **Black Pepper:** 1/4 tsp
- **Lemon Slices:** For garnish

Customizable Ingredients or Garnishes:
- **Fresh Parsley:** 2 tbsp, chopped
- **Red Pepper Flakes:** 1/4 tsp (for a spicy kick)

Instructions:

1. **Preheat the Oven:**
   - Preheat the oven to 375°F (190°C).
2. **Prepare the Marinade:**
   - In a small bowl, whisk together olive oil, lemon juice, minced garlic, fresh thyme, salt, and black pepper.
3. **Marinate the Chicken:**
   - Place the chicken breasts in a baking dish.
   - Pour the marinade over the chicken, ensuring they are evenly coated.
4. **Bake the Chicken:**
   - Bake for 20-25 minutes, or until the chicken is cooked through and the juices run clear.
5. **Serve:**
   - Garnish with lemon slices, fresh parsley, and optional red pepper flakes.
   - Serve immediately.

10. Turkey and Sweet Potato Chili

Yield: 4 servings • Prepration time: 15 Minutes • Cooking Time: 45 Minutes

Ingredients:

- **Ground Turkey:** 1 lb, lean
- **Sweet Potatoes:** 2 cups, diced
- **Onion:** 1, chopped
- **Garlic:** 3 cloves, minced
- **Red Bell Pepper:** 1, diced
- **Tomato Sauce:** 1 can (15 oz)
- **Diced Tomatoes:** 1 can (15 oz)
- **Black Beans:** 1 can (15 oz), drained and rinsed
- **Chicken Broth:** 1 cup, low-sodium
- **Chili Powder:** 2 tbsp
- **Cumin:** 1 tsp
- **Paprika:** 1 tsp
- **Salt:** 1/2 tsp
- **Black Pepper:** 1/4 tsp
- **Olive Oil:** 1 tbsp

Nutritional Information (Per Serving):
- **Calories:** 350
- **Protein:** 30g
- **Carbohydrates:** 40g
- **Fats:** 10g
- **Fiber:** 10g
- **Cholesterol:** 60mg
- **Sodium:** 600mg
- **Potassium:** 1000mg

Customizable Ingredients or Garnishes:
- **Avocado:** 1, diced
- **Fresh Cilantro:** 2 tbsp, chopped
- **Greek Yogurt:** 1/4 cup, low-fat (for serving)

Instructions:

1. **Cook the Turkey:**
   - In a large pot, heat olive oil over medium heat.
   - Add ground turkey and cook until browned, breaking it apart with a spoon.
2. **Add the Vegetables:**
   - Add chopped onion, minced garlic, diced sweet potatoes, and red bell pepper.
   - Cook for 5-7 minutes, until the vegetables are tender.
3. **Add the Remaining Ingredients:**
   - Stir in tomato sauce, diced tomatoes, black beans, chicken broth, chili powder, cumin, paprika, salt, and black pepper.
   - Bring to a boil, then reduce heat and simmer for 30 minutes, until the sweet potatoes are cooked through.
4. **Serve:**
   - Garnish with diced avocado, fresh cilantro, and a dollop of Greek yogurt.
   - Serve immediately.

11. Beef and Broccoli Stir-Fry

> Yield: 4 servings Prepration time: 15 Minutes Cooking Time: 15 Minutes

Nutritional Information (Per Serving):
- **Calories:** 350
- **Protein:** 30g
- **Carbohydrates:** 20g
- **Fats:** 15g
- **Fiber:** 4g
- **Cholesterol:** 75mg
- **Sodium:** 600mg
- **Potassium:** 700mg

Ingredients:

- **Beef Sirloin:** 1 lb, thinly sliced
- **Broccoli Florets:** 4 cups
- **Garlic:** 2 cloves, minced
- **Ginger:** 1 tbsp, minced
- **Soy Sauce:** 3 tbsp, low-sodium
- **Honey:** 1 tbsp
- **Olive Oil:** 2 tbsp
- **Cornstarch:** 1 tbsp (optional, for thickening)
- **Water:** 1/4 cup

Customizable Ingredients or Garnishes:
- **Sesame Seeds:** 1 tbsp
- **Green Onions:** 2 tbsp, sliced
- **Brown Rice:** 2 cups, cooked (for serving)

Instructions:

1. **Prepare the Sauce:**
   - In a small bowl, whisk together soy sauce, honey, and water.
   - If using, mix in cornstarch for thickening.
2. **Cook the Beef:**
   - In a large skillet or wok, heat 1 tbsp olive oil over medium-high heat.
   - Add the beef slices and cook for 2-3 minutes until browned.
   - Remove from the skillet and set aside.
3. **Cook the Vegetables:**
   - In the same skillet, heat the remaining 1 tbsp olive oil.
   - Add minced garlic and ginger, and cook for 1 minute until fragrant.
   - Add broccoli and stir-fry for 3-4 minutes until tender-crisp.
4. **Combine and Serve:**
   - Return the beef to the skillet and pour in the sauce.
   - Stir well to combine and heat through.
5. **Serve:**
   - Garnish with sesame seeds and green onions.
   - Serve with cooked brown rice.

12. Honey Mustard Baked Chicken Thighs

Yield: 4 servings   Prepration time: 10 Minutes   Cooking Time: 35 Minutes

Nutritional Information (Per Serving):
- **Calories:** 280
- **Protein:** 25g
- **Carbohydrates:** 10g
- **Fats:** 15g
- **Fiber:** 1g
- **Cholesterol:** 90mg
- **Sodium:** 400mg
- **Potassium:** 500mg

Ingredients:

- **Chicken Thighs:** 4, bone-in, skinless
- **Honey:** 2 tbsp
- **Dijon Mustard:** 2 tbsp
- **Garlic:** 3 cloves, minced
- **Olive Oil:** 1 tbsp
- **Salt:** 1/2 tsp
- **Black Pepper:** 1/4 tsp
- **Fresh Thyme:** 1 tbsp, chopped

Customizable Ingredients or Garnishes:
- **Fresh Parsley:** 2 tbsp, chopped
- **Red Pepper Flakes:** 1/4 tsp (for a spicy kick)

Instructions:

1. **Preheat the Oven:**
   - Preheat the oven to 375°F (190°C).
2. **Prepare the Marinade:**
   - In a small bowl, whisk together honey, Dijon mustard, minced garlic, olive oil, salt, black pepper, and fresh thyme.
3. **Marinate the Chicken:**
   - Place the chicken thighs in a baking dish.
   - Pour the marinade over the chicken, ensuring they are evenly coated.
4. **Bake the Chicken:**
   - Bake for 30-35 minutes, or until the chicken is cooked through and the juices run clear.
5. **Serve:**
   - Garnish with fresh parsley and optional red pepper flakes.
   - Serve immediately.

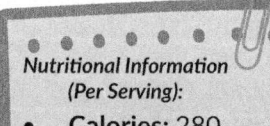

13. Teriyaki Chicken and Vegetable Stir-Fry

Yield: 4 servings Prepration time: 15 Minutes Cooking Time: 15 Minutes

Nutritional Information (Per Serving):
- Calories: 320
- Protein: 30g
- Carbohydrates: 20g
- Fats: 12g
- Fiber: 4g
- Cholesterol: 75mg
- Sodium: 600mg
- Potassium: 700mg

Ingredients:

- **Chicken Breast:** 1 lb, thinly sliced
- **Broccoli Florets:** 2 cups
- **Carrot:** 1, sliced
- **Red Bell Pepper:** 1, sliced
- **Soy Sauce:** 3 tbsp, low-sodium
- **Honey:** 1 tbsp
- **Garlic:** 2 cloves, minced
- **Ginger:** 1 tbsp, minced
- **Olive Oil:** 2 tbsp
- **Cornstarch:** 1 tbsp (optional, for thickening)
- **Water:** 1/4 cup

Customizable Ingredients or Garnishes:
- **Sesame Seeds:** 1 tbsp
- **Green Onions:** 2 tbsp, sliced
- **Brown Rice:** 2 cups, cooked (for serving)

Instructions:

1. **Prepare the Sauce:**
   - In a small bowl, whisk together soy sauce, honey, and water.
   - If using, mix in cornstarch for thickening.
2. **Cook the Chicken:**
   - In a large skillet or wok, heat 1 tbsp olive oil over medium-high heat.
   - Add the chicken slices and cook for 2-3 minutes until browned.
   - Remove from the skillet and set aside.
3. **Cook the Vegetables:**
   - In the same skillet, heat the remaining 1 tbsp olive oil.
   - Add minced garlic and ginger, and cook for 1 minute until fragrant.
   - Add broccoli, carrot, and red bell pepper, and stir-fry for 3-4 minutes until tender-crisp.
4. **Combine and Serve:**
   - Return the chicken to the skillet and pour in the sauce.
   - Stir well to combine and heat through.
5. **Serve:**
   - Garnish with sesame seeds and green onions.
   - Serve with cooked brown rice.

14. Baked Turkey Meatloaf

Yield: 4 servings   Prepration time: 15 Minutes   Cooking Time: 50 Minutes

Ingredients:

- **Ground Turkey:** 1 lb, lean
- **Onion:** 1/2 cup, finely chopped
- **Garlic:** 2 cloves, minced
- **Carrot:** 1, grated
- **Whole Wheat Breadcrumbs:** 1/2 cup
- **Egg:** 1 large
- **Tomato Sauce:** 1/2 cup
- **Worcestershire Sauce:** 1 tbsp
- **Dijon Mustard:** 1 tbsp
- **Salt:** 1/2 tsp
- **Black Pepper:** 1/4 tsp
- **Olive Oil Spray:** For cooking

Nutritional Information (Per Serving):
- **Calories:** 280
- **Protein:** 28g
- **Carbohydrates:** 15g
- **Fats:** 12g
- **Fiber:** 3g
- **Cholesterol:** 90mg
- **Sodium:** 500mg
- **Potassium:** 600mg

Customizable Ingredients or Garnishes:
- **Ketchup:** 1/4 cup (for topping, optional)
- **Fresh Parsley:** 2 tbsp, chopped
- **Red Pepper Flakes:** 1/4 tsp (for a spicy kick)

Instructions:

1. **Preheat the Oven:**
   - Preheat the oven to 375°F (190°C).
   - Spray a loaf pan with olive oil.
2. **Prepare the Meatloaf Mixture:**
   - In a large bowl, combine ground turkey, chopped onion, minced garlic, grated carrot, whole wheat breadcrumbs, egg, tomato sauce, Worcestershire sauce, Dijon mustard, salt, and black pepper.
   - Mix until well combined.
3. **Form the Meatloaf:**
   - Shape the mixture into a loaf and place it in the prepared loaf pan.
4. **Bake the Meatloaf:**
   - If using, spread ketchup over the top of the meatloaf.
   - Bake for 45-50 minutes, or until the meatloaf is cooked through and the internal temperature reaches 165°F (75°C).
5. **Serve:**
   - Garnish with fresh parsley and optional red pepper flakes.
   - Serve immediately.

15. Beef and Vegetable Stuffed Bell Peppers

Yield: 4 servings *Prepration time: 15 Minutes* *Cooking Time: 35 Minutes*

Ingredients:

- **Ground Beef:** 1 lb, lean
- **Bell Peppers:** 4 large, tops cut off and seeds removed
- **Onion:** 1, chopped
- **Garlic:** 2 cloves, minced
- **Tomato Sauce:** 1 cup, low-sodium
- **Brown Rice:** 1 cup, cooked
- **Carrot:** 1, grated
- **Zucchini:** 1, grated
- **Salt:** 1/2 tsp
- **Black Pepper:** 1/4 tsp
- **Olive Oil:** 1 tbsp
- **Fresh Parsley:** 2 tbsp, chopped (for garnish)

Nutritional Information (Per Serving):
- Calories: 300
- Protein: 25g
- Carbohydrates: 25g
- Fats: 12g
- Fiber: 5g
- Cholesterol: 60mg
- Sodium: 500mg
- Potassium: 800mg

Customizable Ingredients or Garnishes:
- **Parmesan Cheese:** 1/4 cup, grated (optional)
- **Red Pepper Flakes:** 1/4 tsp (for a spicy kick)

Instructions:

1. **Preheat the Oven:**
   - Preheat the oven to 375°F (190°C).
2. **Cook the Beef:**
   - In a skillet, heat olive oil over medium heat.
   - Add ground beef, chopped onion, and minced garlic. Cook until the beef is browned and the onion is soft.
3. **Add Vegetables and Sauce:**
   - Stir in grated carrot, grated zucchini, tomato sauce, salt, and black pepper.
   - Simmer for 5 minutes.
4. **Stuff the Peppers:**
   - Mix the cooked brown rice into the beef and vegetable mixture.
   - Stuff the bell peppers with the mixture and place them in a baking dish.
5. **Bake the Peppers:**
   - Cover with foil and bake for 30-35 minutes, or until the peppers are tender.
6. **Serve:**
   - Garnish with fresh parsley and optional Parmesan cheese and red pepper flakes.
   - Serve immediately.

16. Chicken and Zucchini Noodles

Yield: 4 servings   Prepration time: 15 Minutes   Cooking Time: 15 Minutes

Ingredients:

- **Chicken Breast:** 1 lb, thinly sliced
- **Zucchini:** 4, spiralized into noodles
- **Garlic:** 3 cloves, minced
- **Cherry Tomatoes:** 1 cup, halved
- **Olive Oil:** 2 tbsp
- **Lemon Juice:** 2 tbsp
- **Fresh Basil:** 1/4 cup, chopped
- **Salt:** 1/2 tsp
- **Black Pepper:** 1/4 tsp

Customizable Ingredients or Garnishes:
- **Parmesan Cheese:** 1/4 cup, grated (optional)
- **Red Pepper Flakes:** 1/4 tsp (for a spicy kick)

Nutritional Information (Per Serving):
- **Calories:** 250
- **Protein:** 30g
- **Carbohydrates:** 10g
- **Fats:** 10g
- **Fiber:** 3g
- **Cholesterol:** 75mg
- **Sodium:** 400mg
- **Potassium:** 700mg

Instructions:

1. **Cook the Chicken:**
   - In a large skillet, heat 1 tbsp olive oil over medium-high heat.
   - Add the thinly sliced chicken breast and cook for 5-7 minutes until browned and cooked through.
   - Remove from skillet and set aside.
2. **Cook the Vegetables:**
   - In the same skillet, heat the remaining 1 tbsp olive oil.
   - Add minced garlic and cook for 1 minute until fragrant.
   - Add cherry tomatoes and cook for 2-3 minutes until they begin to soften.
3. **Add the Zucchini Noodles:**
   - Add the spiralized zucchini noodles to the skillet.
   - Cook for 3-4 minutes until tender but still firm.
4. **Combine and Serve:**
   - Return the cooked chicken to the skillet.
   - Stir in lemon juice, fresh basil, salt, and black pepper.
   - Garnish with optional Parmesan cheese and red pepper flakes.
   - Serve immediately.

17. Herb-Crusted Roast Beef

Yield: 4 servings **Prepration time:** 10 Minutes **Cooking Time:** 1 Hour

Nutritional Information (Per Serving):
- Calories: 320
- Protein: 30g
- Carbohydrates: 2g
- Fats: 20g
- Fiber: 0g
- Cholesterol: 80mg
- Sodium: 400mg
- Potassium: 500mg

Ingredients:

- **Beef Tenderloin:** 1 lb
- **Olive Oil:** 2 tbsp
- **Garlic:** 4 cloves, minced
- **Fresh Rosemary:** 2 tbsp, chopped
- **Fresh Thyme:** 2 tbsp, chopped
- **Salt:** 1/2 tsp
- **Black Pepper:** 1/4 tsp

Customizable Ingredients or Garnishes:
- **Red Wine Sauce:** 1/2 cup (for serving)
- **Fresh Parsley:** 2 tbsp, chopped

Instructions:

1. **Preheat the Oven:**
   - Preheat the oven to 375°F (190°C).
2. **Prepare the Herb Crust:**
   - In a small bowl, mix together olive oil, minced garlic, fresh rosemary, fresh thyme, salt, and black pepper.
3. **Coat the Beef:**
   - Rub the herb mixture over the beef tenderloin.
4. **Roast the Beef:**
   - Place the beef in a roasting pan and roast for 50-60 minutes, or until the internal temperature reaches 135°F (57°C) for medium-rare.
5. **Rest and Serve:**
   - Let the beef rest for 10 minutes before slicing.
   - Serve with red wine sauce and garnish with fresh parsley.

18. Grilled Chicken Caesar Salad

Yield: 4 servings *Prepration time: 15 Minutes* *Cooking Time: 10 Minutes*

Ingredients:

- **Chicken Breast:** 1 lb, thinly sliced
- **Romaine Lettuce:** 4 cups, chopped
- **Cherry Tomatoes:** 1 cup, halved
- **Parmesan Cheese:** 1/4 cup, shaved
- **Whole Wheat Croutons:** 1 cup
- **Caesar Dressing:** 1/4 cup, low-fat

Customizable Ingredients or Garnishes:
- **Lemon Wedges:** For serving
- **Fresh Basil:** 2 tbsp, chopped

Nutritional Information (Per Serving):
- **Calories:** 300
- **Protein:** 30g
- **Carbohydrates:** 20g
- **Fats:** 12g
- **Fiber:** 5g
- **Cholesterol:** 75mg
- **Sodium:** 600mg
- **Potassium:** 700mg

Instructions:

1. **Grill the Chicken:**
   - Preheat the grill to medium-high heat.
   - Grill the thinly sliced chicken breast for 4-5 minutes per side, or until cooked through.
   - Remove from grill and let rest for a few minutes before slicing.
2. **Prepare the Salad:**
   - In a large bowl, combine chopped romaine lettuce, halved cherry tomatoes, shaved Parmesan cheese, and whole wheat croutons.
3. **Add the Chicken:**
   - Add the sliced grilled chicken to the salad.
4. **Serve:**
   - Drizzle with low-fat Caesar dressing.
   - Garnish with lemon wedges and fresh basil if desired.
   - Serve immediately.

19. Sesame Chicken and Broccoli

Yield: 4 servings Prepration time: 15 Minutes Cooking Time: 15 Minutes

Nutritional Information (Per Serving):
- Calories: 320
- Protein: 30g
- Carbohydrates: 20g
- Fats: 12g
- Fiber: 4g
- Cholesterol: 75mg
- Sodium: 600mg
- Potassium: 700mg

Ingredients:

- **Chicken Breast:** 1 lb, thinly sliced
- **Broccoli Florets:** 4 cups
- **Garlic:** 2 cloves, minced
- **Soy Sauce:** 3 tbsp, low-sodium
- **Honey:** 1 tbsp
- **Sesame Oil:** 1 tbsp
- **Olive Oil:** 2 tbsp
- **Sesame Seeds:** 1 tbsp
- **Cornstarch:** 1 tbsp (optional, for thickening)
- **Water:** 1/4 cup

Customizable Ingredients or Garnishes:
- **Green Onions:** 2 tbsp, sliced
- **Red Pepper Flakes:** 1/4 tsp (for a spicy kick)
- **Brown Rice:** 2 cups, cooked (for serving)

Instructions:

1. **Prepare the Sauce:**
   - In a small bowl, whisk together soy sauce, honey, sesame oil, and water.
   - If using, mix in cornstarch for thickening.
2. **Cook the Chicken:**
   - In a large skillet or wok, heat 1 tbsp olive oil over medium-high heat.
   - Add the chicken slices and cook for 2-3 minutes until browned.
   - Remove from the skillet and set aside.
3. **Cook the Broccoli:**
   - In the same skillet, heat the remaining 1 tbsp olive oil.
   - Add minced garlic and cook for 1 minute until fragrant.
   - Add broccoli and stir-fry for 3-4 minutes until tender-crisp.
4. **Combine and Serve:**
   - Return the chicken to the skillet and pour in the sauce.
   - Stir well to combine and heat through.
   - Garnish with sesame seeds and green onions.
   - Serve with cooked brown rice.

20. Beef and Mushroom Lettuce Wraps

Yield: 4 servings   Prepration time: 15 Minutes   Cooking Time: 10 Minutes

Ingredients:

- **Ground Beef:** 1 lb, lean
- **Mushrooms:** 2 cups, chopped
- **Onion:** 1, finely chopped
- **Garlic:** 2 cloves, minced
- **Soy Sauce:** 3 tbsp, low-sodium
- **Hoisin Sauce:** 2 tbsp
- **Olive Oil:** 1 tbsp
- **Romaine Lettuce Leaves:** 8 large

Customizable Ingredients or Garnishes:
- **Green Onions:** 2 tbsp, sliced
- **Cilantro:** 2 tbsp, chopped
- **Lime Wedges:** For serving

Nutritional Information (Per Serving):
- Calories: 250
- Protein: 25g
- Carbohydrates: 10g
- Fats: 12g
- Fiber: 3g
- Cholesterol: 70mg
- Sodium: 550mg
- Potassium: 500mg

Instructions:

1. **Cook the Beef:**
   - In a skillet, heat olive oil over medium heat.
   - Add ground beef, chopped mushrooms, and finely chopped onion. Cook until the beef is browned and the vegetables are tender.
2. **Add the Sauce:**
   - Stir in minced garlic, soy sauce, and hoisin sauce.
   - Cook for an additional 2 minutes until heated through.
3. **Assemble the Lettuce Wraps:**
   - Spoon the beef and mushroom mixture into the center of each romaine lettuce leaf.
4. **Serve:**
   - Garnish with green onions and cilantro.
   - Serve with lime wedges.

CHAPTER 5. SIDES AND VEGETABLES

1. Garlic Roasted Brussels Sprouts

Yield: 4 servings Prepration time: 10 Minutes Cooking Time: 25 Minutes

Nutritional Information (Per Serving):
- Calories: 120
- Protein: 3g
- Carbohydrates: 12g
- Fats: 7g
- Fiber: 4g
- Cholesterol: 0mg
- Sodium: 300mg
- Potassium: 450mg

Ingredients:

- **Brussels Sprouts:** 1 lb, trimmed and halved
- **Olive Oil:** 2 tbsp
- **Garlic:** 3 cloves, minced
- **Salt:** 1/2 tsp
- **Black Pepper:** 1/4 tsp

Customizable Ingredients or Garnishes:
- **Lemon Zest:** 1 tsp (for added flavor)
- **Parmesan Cheese:** 1/4 cup, grated (optional)
- **Red Pepper Flakes:** 1/4 tsp (for a spicy kick)

Instructions:

1. **Preheat the Oven:**
   - Preheat the oven to 400°F (200°C).
2. **Prepare the Brussels Sprouts:**
   - In a large bowl, combine Brussels sprouts, olive oil, minced garlic, salt, and black pepper.
   - Toss to coat evenly.
3. **Roast the Brussels Sprouts:**
   - Spread the Brussels sprouts in a single layer on a baking sheet.
   - Roast for 20-25 minutes, stirring halfway through, until tender and golden brown.
4. **Serve:**
   - Garnish with lemon zest, Parmesan cheese, and optional red pepper flakes if desired.
   - Serve immediately.

2. Quinoa and Black Bean Salad

Yield: 4 servings Prepration time: 15 Minutes Cooking Time: 15 Minutes

Ingredients:

- **Quinoa:** 1 cup, uncooked
- **Black Beans:** 1 can (15 oz), drained and rinsed
- **Corn Kernels:** 1 cup, cooked
- **Red Bell Pepper:** 1, diced
- **Red Onion:** 1/4 cup, finely chopped
- **Cherry Tomatoes:** 1 cup, halved
- **Cilantro:** 1/4 cup, chopped
- **Olive Oil:** 2 tbsp
- **Lime Juice:** 2 tbsp
- **Cumin:** 1 tsp
- **Salt:** 1/2 tsp
- **Black Pepper:** 1/4 tsp

Nutritional Information (Per Serving):
- **Calories:** 250
- **Protein:** 8g
- **Carbohydrates:** 40g
- **Fats:** 7g
- **Fiber:** 9g
- **Cholesterol:** 0mg
- **Sodium:** 400mg
- **Potassium:** 600mg

Customizable Ingredients or Garnishes:
- **Avocado:** 1, diced
- **Feta Cheese:** 1/4 cup, crumbled (optional)
- **Red Pepper Flakes:** 1/4 tsp (for a spicy kick)

Instructions:

1. **Cook the Quinoa:**
    - Rinse the quinoa under cold water.
    - In a medium pot, bring 2 cups of water to a boil.
    - Add the quinoa, reduce heat to low, cover, and simmer for 15 minutes, or until the quinoa is cooked and the water is absorbed.
    - Fluff with a fork and let cool.
2. **Prepare the Salad:**
    - In a large bowl, combine cooked quinoa, black beans, corn, diced red bell pepper, chopped red onion, halved cherry tomatoes, and chopped cilantro.
3. **Make the Dressing:**
    - In a small bowl, whisk together olive oil, lime juice, cumin, salt, and black pepper.
4. **Assemble the Salad:**
    - Pour the dressing over the quinoa mixture and toss to combine.
5. **Serve:**
    - Garnish with diced avocado, optional feta cheese, and red pepper flakes.
    - Serve immediately or refrigerate until ready to serve.

3. Balsamic Glazed Carrots

Yield: 4 servings   Prepration time: 10 Minutes   Cooking Time: 25 Minutes

Ingredients:

- **Carrots:** 1 lb, peeled and sliced
- **Olive Oil:** 1 tbsp
- **Balsamic Vinegar:** 2 tbsp
- **Honey:** 1 tbsp
- **Garlic:** 2 cloves, minced
- **Salt:** 1/2 tsp
- **Black Pepper:** 1/4 tsp

Customizable Ingredients or Garnishes:
- **Fresh Thyme:** 1 tbsp, chopped (for added flavor)
- **Red Pepper Flakes:** 1/4 tsp (for a spicy kick)

Nutritional Information (Per Serving):
- Calories: 120
- Protein: 1g
- Carbohydrates: 18g
- Fats: 5g
- Fiber: 3g
- Cholesterol: 0mg
- Sodium: 300mg
- Potassium: 450mg

Instructions:

1. **Preheat the Oven:**
   - Preheat the oven to 400°F (200°C).
2. **Prepare the Carrots:**
   - In a large bowl, combine sliced carrots, olive oil, balsamic vinegar, honey, minced garlic, salt, and black pepper.
   - Toss to coat evenly.
3. **Roast the Carrots:**
   - Spread the carrots in a single layer on a baking sheet.
   - Roast for 20-25 minutes, stirring halfway through, until tender and caramelized.
4. **Serve:**
   - Garnish with fresh thyme and optional red pepper flakes if desired.
   - Serve immediately.

4. Cauliflower Rice Pilaf

Yield: 4 servings   *Prepration time: 10 Minutes*   *Cooking Time: 15 Minutes*

Ingredients:

- **Cauliflower:** 1 head, grated into rice-sized pieces
- **Olive Oil:** 2 tbsp
- **Onion:** 1, finely chopped
- **Garlic:** 2 cloves, minced
- **Carrot:** 1, grated
- **Peas:** 1 cup, cooked
- **Vegetable Broth:** 1/4 cup, low-sodium
- **Salt:** 1/2 tsp
- **Black Pepper:** 1/4 tsp
- **Fresh Parsley:** 2 tbsp, chopped (for garnish)

Customizable Ingredients or Garnishes:
- **Lemon Juice:** 1 tbsp (for added flavor)
- **Sliced Almonds:** 1/4 cup (for crunch)

Nutritional Information (Per Serving):
- **Calories:** 100
- **Protein:** 3g
- **Carbohydrates:** 15g
- **Fats:** 5g
- **Fiber:** 4g
- **Cholesterol:** 0mg
- **Sodium:** 300mg
- **Potassium:** 400mg

Instructions:

1. **Prepare the Cauliflower:**
   - Grate the cauliflower using a food processor or a box grater until it resembles rice-sized pieces.
2. **Cook the Vegetables:**
   - In a large skillet, heat olive oil over medium heat.
   - Add chopped onion and minced garlic, and cook for 2-3 minutes until softened.
   - Add grated carrot and cook for another 2 minutes.
3. **Cook the Cauliflower:**
   - Add the grated cauliflower and vegetable broth to the skillet.
   - Cook for 5-7 minutes, stirring frequently, until the cauliflower is tender.
4. **Add the Peas:**
   - Stir in the cooked peas, salt, and black pepper.
   - Cook for an additional 2 minutes.
5. **Serve:**
   - Garnish with fresh parsley, lemon juice, and optional sliced almonds.
   - Serve immediately.

5. Sautéed Spinach with Garlic

Yield: 4 servings **Prepration time:** 5 Minutes **Cooking Time:** 5 Minutes

Ingredients:

- **Spinach:** 1 lb, fresh
- **Olive Oil:** 1 tbsp
- **Garlic:** 3 cloves, minced
- **Salt:** 1/2 tsp
- **Black Pepper:** 1/4 tsp

Customizable Ingredients or Garnishes:
- **Lemon Juice:** 1 tbsp (for added flavor)
- **Red Pepper Flakes:** 1/4 tsp (for a spicy kick)

Nutritional Information (Per Serving):
- Calories: 60
- Protein: 3g
- Carbohydrates: 5g
- Fats: 4g
- Fiber: 3g
- Cholesterol: 0mg
- Sodium: 300mg
- Potassium: 500mg

Instructions:

1. **Prepare the Spinach:**
   - Rinse the spinach and remove any tough stems.
2. **Cook the Garlic:**
   - In a large skillet, heat olive oil over medium heat.
   - Add minced garlic and cook for 1 minute until fragrant.
3. **Add the Spinach:**
   - Add the spinach to the skillet, stirring frequently until wilted, about 3-4 minutes.
4. **Season and Serve:**
   - Season with salt and black pepper.
   - Garnish with lemon juice and optional red pepper flakes.
   - Serve immediately.

6. Sweet Potato and Kale Hash

Yield: 4 servings Prepration time: 10 Minutes Cooking Time: 20 Minutes

Ingredients:

- **Sweet Potatoes:** 2 large, peeled and diced
- **Kale:** 4 cups, chopped
- **Olive Oil:** 2 tbsp
- **Onion:** 1, chopped
- **Garlic:** 2 cloves, minced
- **Paprika:** 1 tsp
- **Salt:** 1/2 tsp
- **Black Pepper:** 1/4 tsp

Customizable Ingredients or Garnishes:
- **Red Bell Pepper:** 1, diced (for added color)
- **Fresh Parsley:** 2 tbsp, chopped (for garnish)
- **Feta Cheese:** 1/4 cup, crumbled (optional)

Nutritional Information (Per Serving):
- **Calories:** 180
- **Protein:** 4g
- **Carbohydrates:** 30g
- **Fats:** 7g
- **Fiber:** 6g
- **Cholesterol:** 0mg
- **Sodium:** 350mg
- **Potassium:** 800mg

Instructions:

1. **Cook the Sweet Potatoes:**
   - In a large skillet, heat 1 tbsp of olive oil over medium heat.
   - Add diced sweet potatoes and cook for 10-12 minutes, stirring occasionally, until tender.
2. **Add the Vegetables:**
   - Add the remaining 1 tbsp of olive oil to the skillet.
   - Stir in chopped onion, minced garlic, and diced red bell pepper (if using).
   - Cook for 3-4 minutes until the onion is softened.
3. **Add the Kale:**
   - Add the chopped kale to the skillet.
   - Cook for 2-3 minutes until wilted.
4. **Season and Serve:**
   - Season with paprika, salt, and black pepper.
   - Garnish with fresh parsley and optional feta cheese.
   - Serve immediately.

7. Roasted Beet and Arugula Salad

Yield: 4 servings | Prepration time: 10 Minutes | Cooking Time: 45 Minutes

Ingredients:

- **Beets:** 4 medium, peeled and diced
- **Olive Oil:** 2 tbsp
- **Salt:** 1/2 tsp
- **Black Pepper:** 1/4 tsp
- **Arugula:** 4 cups, fresh
- **Goat Cheese:** 1/4 cup, crumbled (optional)
- **Balsamic Vinegar:** 2 tbsp

Customizable Ingredients or Garnishes:
- **Walnuts:** 1/4 cup, toasted (for added crunch)
- **Red Onion:** 1/4 cup, thinly sliced (for added flavor)

Nutritional Information (Per Serving):
- **Calories:** 150
- **Protein:** 4g
- **Carbohydrates:** 15g
- **Fats:** 9g
- **Fiber:** 4g
- **Cholesterol:** 5mg
- **Sodium:** 300mg
- **Potassium:** 500mg

Instructions:

1. **Preheat the Oven:**
   - Preheat the oven to 400°F (200°C).
2. **Roast the Beets:**
   - In a bowl, toss the diced beets with olive oil, salt, and black pepper.
   - Spread the beets on a baking sheet and roast for 40-45 minutes, stirring halfway through, until tender.
3. **Prepare the Salad:**
   - In a large bowl, combine fresh arugula, roasted beets, crumbled goat cheese (if using), and toasted walnuts (if using).
4. **Add the Dressing:**
   - Drizzle with balsamic vinegar and toss to combine.
5. **Serve:**
   - Garnish with thinly sliced red onion (if using).
   - Serve immediately.

8. Lemon Garlic Asparagus

Yield: 4 servings Prepration time: 5 Minutes Cooking Time: 10 Minutes

Nutritional Information (Per Serving):
- **Calories:** 80
- **Protein:** 3g
- **Carbohydrates:** 7g
- **Fats:** 5g
- **Fiber:** 3g
- **Cholesterol:** 0mg
- **Sodium:** 250mg
- **Potassium:** 300mg

Ingredients:

- **Asparagus:** 1 lb, trimmed
- **Olive Oil:** 1 tbsp
- **Garlic:** 2 cloves, minced
- **Lemon Juice:** 1 tbsp
- **Lemon Zest:** 1 tsp
- **Salt:** 1/2 tsp
- **Black Pepper:** 1/4 tsp

Customizable Ingredients or Garnishes:
- **Parmesan Cheese:** 1/4 cup, grated (optional)
- **Red Pepper Flakes:** 1/4 tsp (for a spicy kick)

Instructions:

1. **Prepare the Asparagus:**
   - Rinse and trim the asparagus.
2. **Cook the Asparagus:**
   - In a large skillet, heat olive oil over medium heat.
   - Add minced garlic and cook for 1 minute until fragrant.
   - Add the asparagus and cook for 5-7 minutes, stirring occasionally, until tender-crisp.
3. **Season and Serve:**
   - Add lemon juice, lemon zest, salt, and black pepper.
   - Garnish with optional Parmesan cheese and red pepper flakes.
   - Serve immediately.

9. Grilled Vegetable Medley

Yield: 4 servings   Prepration time: 10 Minutes   Cooking Time: 15 Minutes

Ingredients:

- **Zucchini:** 2, sliced
- **Red Bell Pepper:** 1, cut into strips
- **Yellow Bell Pepper:** 1, cut into strips
- **Red Onion:** 1, cut into wedges
- **Mushrooms:** 1 cup, halved
- **Olive Oil:** 2 tbsp
- **Balsamic Vinegar:** 1 tbsp
- **Garlic:** 2 cloves, minced
- **Salt:** 1/2 tsp
- **Black Pepper:** 1/4 tsp

Customizable Ingredients or Garnishes:
- **Fresh Basil:** 2 tbsp, chopped
- **Lemon Juice:** 1 tbsp (for added flavor)
- **Red Pepper Flakes:** 1/4 tsp (for a spicy kick)

Nutritional Information (Per Serving):
- **Calories:** 100
- **Protein:** 2g
- **Carbohydrates:** 10g
- **Fats:** 7g
- **Fiber:** 3g
- **Cholesterol:** 0mg
- **Sodium:** 200mg
- **Potassium:** 400mg

Instructions:

1. **Preheat the Grill:**
   - Preheat the grill to medium-high heat.
2. **Prepare the Vegetables:**
   - In a large bowl, combine sliced zucchini, bell peppers, red onion, and mushrooms.
   - Add olive oil, balsamic vinegar, minced garlic, salt, and black pepper.
   - Toss to coat evenly.
3. **Grill the Vegetables:**
   - Place the vegetables in a grill basket or directly on the grill grates.
   - Grill for 10-15 minutes, turning occasionally, until tender and slightly charred.
4. **Serve:**
   - Garnish with fresh basil, lemon juice, and optional red pepper flakes.
   - Serve immediately.

10. Chickpea and Tomato Salad

Yield: 4 servings   Prepration time: 10 Minutes   Cooking Time: 0 Minutes

Ingredients:

- **Chickpeas:** 1 can (15 oz), drained and rinsed
- **Cherry Tomatoes:** 1 cup, halved
- **Cucumber:** 1, diced
- **Red Onion:** 1/4 cup, finely chopped
- **Olive Oil:** 2 tbsp
- **Lemon Juice:** 2 tbsp
- **Fresh Parsley:** 2 tbsp, chopped
- **Salt:** 1/2 tsp
- **Black Pepper:** 1/4 tsp

Customizable Ingredients or Garnishes:
- **Feta Cheese:** 1/4 cup, crumbled (optional)
- **Avocado:** 1, diced
- **Red Pepper Flakes:** 1/4 tsp (for a spicy kick)

Nutritional Information (Per Serving):
- **Calories:** 180
- **Protein:** 6g
- **Carbohydrates:** 22g
- **Fats:** 8g
- **Fiber:** 6g
- **Cholesterol:** 0mg
- **Sodium:** 350mg
- **Potassium:** 400mg

Instructions:

1. **Prepare the Salad:**
   - In a large bowl, combine chickpeas, halved cherry tomatoes, diced cucumber, and finely chopped red onion.
2. **Make the Dressing:**
   - In a small bowl, whisk together olive oil, lemon juice, fresh parsley, salt, and black pepper.
3. **Assemble the Salad:**
   - Pour the dressing over the chickpea mixture and toss to combine.
4. **Serve:**
   - Garnish with optional feta cheese, avocado, and red pepper flakes.
   - Serve immediately or refrigerate until ready to serve.

11. Spaghetti Squash with Marinara Sauce

Yield: 4 servings | Prepration time: 10 Minutes | Cooking Time: 40 Minutes

Ingredients:

- **Spaghetti Squash:** 1 large
- **Olive Oil:** 1 tbsp
- **Salt:** 1/2 tsp
- **Black Pepper:** 1/4 tsp
- **Marinara Sauce:** 2 cups, low-sodium

Customizable Ingredients or Garnishes:
- **Parmesan Cheese:** 1/4 cup, grated (optional)
- **Fresh Basil:** 2 tbsp, chopped
- **Red Pepper Flakes:** 1/4 tsp (for a spicy kick)

Nutritional Information (Per Serving):
- **Calories:** 120
- **Protein:** 3g
- **Carbohydrates:** 20g
- **Fats:** 5g
- **Fiber:** 4g
- **Cholesterol:** 0mg
- **Sodium:** 400mg
- **Potassium:** 500mg

Instructions:

1. **Preheat the Oven:**
   - Preheat the oven to 400°F (200°C).
2. **Prepare the Spaghetti Squash:**
   - Cut the spaghetti squash in half lengthwise and remove the seeds.
   - Drizzle with olive oil and season with salt and black pepper.
   - Place cut-side down on a baking sheet and roast for 35-40 minutes, until tender.
3. **Prepare the Marinara Sauce:**
   - In a saucepan, heat the marinara sauce over medium heat until warmed through.
4. **Serve:**
   - Use a fork to scrape the spaghetti squash strands into a serving dish.
   - Top with marinara sauce and garnish with optional Parmesan cheese, fresh basil, and red pepper flakes.
   - Serve immediately.

12. Steamed Broccoli with Lemon Zest

Yield: 4 servings Prepration time: 5 Minutes Cooking Time: 10 Minutes

Ingredients:

- **Broccoli Florets:** 4 cups
- **Olive Oil:** 1 tbsp
- **Lemon Zest:** 1 tsp
- **Lemon Juice:** 1 tbsp
- **Salt:** 1/2 tsp
- **Black Pepper:** 1/4 tsp

Customizable Ingredients or Garnishes:
- **Parmesan Cheese:** 1/4 cup, grated (optional)
- **Red Pepper Flakes:** 1/4 tsp (for a spicy kick)

Nutritional Information (Per Serving):
- **Calories:** 80
- **Protein:** 3g
- **Carbohydrates:** 7g
- **Fats:** 5g
- **Fiber:** 3g
- **Cholesterol:** 0mg
- **Sodium:** 250mg
- **Potassium:** 300mg

Instructions:

1. **Steam the Broccoli:**
   - In a steamer basket, steam broccoli florets for 5-7 minutes until tender-crisp.
2. **Prepare the Dressing:**
   - In a small bowl, whisk together olive oil, lemon zest, lemon juice, salt, and black pepper.
3. **Serve:**
   - Drizzle the dressing over the steamed broccoli.
   - Garnish with optional Parmesan cheese and red pepper flakes.
   - Serve immediately.

13. Roasted Butternut Squash with Sage

Yield: 4 servings Prepration time: 10 Minutes Cooking Time: 35 Minutes

Ingredients:

- **Butternut Squash:** 1 large, peeled and cubed
- **Olive Oil:** 2 tbsp
- **Fresh Sage:** 2 tbsp, chopped
- **Salt:** 1/2 tsp
- **Black Pepper:** 1/4 tsp

Customizable Ingredients or Garnishes:
- **Maple Syrup:** 1 tbsp (for added sweetness)
- **Red Pepper Flakes:** 1/4 tsp (for a spicy kick)

Nutritional Information (Per Serving):
- **Calories:** 150
- **Protein:** 2g
- **Carbohydrates:** 25g
- **Fats:** 7g
- **Fiber:** 4g
- **Cholesterol:** 0mg
- **Sodium:** 300mg
- **Potassium:** 450mg

Instructions:

1. **Preheat the Oven:**
   - Preheat the oven to 400°F (200°C).
2. **Prepare the Squash:**
   - In a large bowl, combine cubed butternut squash, olive oil, chopped sage, salt, and black pepper.
   - Toss to coat evenly.
3. **Roast the Squash:**
   - Spread the squash in a single layer on a baking sheet.
   - Roast for 30-35 minutes, stirring halfway through, until tender and caramelized.
4. **Serve:**
   - Garnish with optional maple syrup and red pepper flakes.
   - Serve immediately.

14. Zucchini Noodles with Pesto

Yield: 4 servings *Prepration time: 10 Minutes* *Cooking Time: 5 Minutes*

Ingredients:

- **Zucchini:** 4, spiralized into noodles
- **Olive Oil:** 2 tbsp
- **Garlic:** 2 cloves, minced
- **Basil Pesto:** 1/4 cup, low-fat
- **Salt:** 1/2 tsp
- **Black Pepper:** 1/4 tsp

Customizable Ingredients or Garnishes:
- **Cherry Tomatoes:** 1 cup, halved (for added color)
- **Parmesan Cheese:** 1/4 cup, grated (optional)
- **Red Pepper Flakes:** 1/4 tsp (for a spicy kick)

Nutritional Information (Per Serving):
- **Calories:** 120
- **Protein:** 3g
- **Carbohydrates:** 10g
- **Fats:** 8g
- **Fiber:** 2g
- **Cholesterol:** 0mg
- **Sodium:** 300mg
- **Potassium:** 450mg

Instructions:

1. **Prepare the Zucchini:**
   - Spiralize the zucchini into noodles using a spiralizer or a julienne peeler.
2. **Cook the Zucchini Noodles:**
   - In a large skillet, heat olive oil over medium heat.
   - Add minced garlic and cook for 1 minute until fragrant.
   - Add the zucchini noodles and cook for 2-3 minutes until tender but still firm.
3. **Add the Pesto:**
   - Stir in the basil pesto, salt, and black pepper.
   - Cook for an additional 1-2 minutes until heated through.
4. **Serve:**
   - Garnish with optional cherry tomatoes, Parmesan cheese, and red pepper flakes.
   - Serve immediately.

15. Cucumber and Dill Salad

Yield: 4 servings Prepration time: 10 Minutes Cooking Time: 0 Minutes

Ingredients:

- **Cucumber:** 2 large, thinly sliced
- **Red Onion:** 1/4 cup, thinly sliced
- **Greek Yogurt:** 1/2 cup, low-fat
- **Fresh Dill:** 2 tbsp, chopped
- **Lemon Juice:** 1 tbsp
- **Salt:** 1/2 tsp
- **Black Pepper:** 1/4 tsp

Customizable Ingredients or Garnishes:
- **Avocado:** 1, diced (for added creaminess)
- **Cherry Tomatoes:** 1 cup, halved (for added color)
- **Red Pepper Flakes:** 1/4 tsp (for a spicy kick)

Nutritional Information (Per Serving):
- Calories: 60
- Protein: 3g
- Carbohydrates: 10g
- Fats: 2g
- Fiber: 2g
- Cholesterol: 0mg
- Sodium: 250mg
- Potassium: 350mg

Instructions:

1. **Prepare the Salad:**
   - In a large bowl, combine thinly sliced cucumber and red onion.
2. **Make the Dressing:**
   - In a small bowl, whisk together Greek yogurt, fresh dill, lemon juice, salt, and black pepper.
3. **Assemble the Salad:**
   - Pour the dressing over the cucumber mixture and toss to combine.
4. **Serve:**
   - Garnish with optional avocado, cherry tomatoes, and red pepper flakes.
   - Serve immediately or refrigerate until ready to serve.

CHAPTER 6. SOUPS

1. Tomato Basil Soup

Yield: 4 servings *Prepration time: 10 Minutes* *Cooking Time: 30 Minutes*

Nutritional Information (Per Serving):
- **Calories:** 120
- **Protein:** 2g
- **Carbohydrates:** 20g
- **Fats:** 5g
- **Fiber:** 4g
- **Cholesterol:** 0mg
- **Sodium:** 250mg
- **Potassium:** 500mg

Ingredients:

- **Olive Oil:** 2 tbsp
- **Onion:** 1, chopped
- **Garlic:** 3 cloves, minced
- **Tomatoes:** 6 large, chopped (or 2 cans of diced tomatoes, 28 oz each)
- **Vegetable Broth:** 4 cups, low-sodium
- **Tomato Paste:** 2 tbsp
- **Fresh Basil:** 1/4 cup, chopped
- **Salt:** 1/2 tsp
- **Black Pepper:** 1/4 tsp
- **Balsamic Vinegar:** 1 tbsp (optional, for added depth of flavor)

Customizable Ingredients or Garnishes:
- **Fresh Basil Leaves:** For garnish
- **Greek Yogurt:** 1/4 cup, low-fat (for a creamy texture)
- **Red Pepper Flakes:** 1/4 tsp (for a spicy kick)

Instructions:

1. **Cook the Vegetables:**
   - In a large pot, heat olive oil over medium heat.
   - Add chopped onion and cook for 5 minutes until softened.
   - Add minced garlic and cook for another minute.
2. **Add Tomatoes and Broth:**
   - Add chopped tomatoes (or canned tomatoes), vegetable broth, and tomato paste.
   - Bring to a boil, then reduce heat and simmer for 20 minutes.
3. **Blend the Soup:**
   - Using an immersion blender or regular blender, blend the soup until smooth.
   - Return to the pot and stir in chopped basil, salt, black pepper, and optional balsamic vinegar.
   - Simmer for an additional 5 minutes.
4. **Serve:**
   - Garnish with fresh basil leaves, a dollop of Greek yogurt, and optional red pepper flakes.
   - Serve immediately.

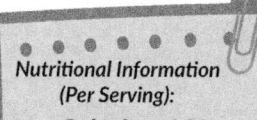

2. Chickpea and Spinach Soup

Yield: 4 servings Prepration time: 10 Minutes Cooking Time: 30 Minutes

Ingredients:

- **Olive Oil:** 2 tbsp
- **Onion:** 1, chopped
- **Garlic:** 3 cloves, minced
- **Carrot:** 1, diced
- **Celery:** 2 stalks, diced
- **Chickpeas:** 1 can (15 oz), drained and rinsed
- **Vegetable Broth:** 4 cups, low-sodium
- **Diced Tomatoes:** 1 can (15 oz)
- **Fresh Spinach:** 4 cups
- **Cumin:** 1 tsp
- **Paprika:** 1 tsp
- **Salt:** 1/2 tsp
- **Black Pepper:** 1/4 tsp
- **Lemon Juice:** 1 tbsp

Nutritional Information (Per Serving):
- **Calories:** 180
- **Protein:** 6g
- **Carbohydrates:** 25g
- **Fats:** 7g
- **Fiber:** 6g
- **Cholesterol:** 0mg
- **Sodium:** 300mg
- **Potassium:** 600mg

Customizable Ingredients or Garnishes:
- **Fresh Parsley:** For garnish
- **Red Pepper Flakes:** 1/4 tsp (for a spicy kick)
- **Greek Yogurt:** 1/4 cup, low-fat (for added creaminess)

Instructions:

1. **Cook the Vegetables:**
   - In a large pot, heat olive oil over medium heat.
   - Add chopped onion, diced carrot, and diced celery. Cook for 5 minutes until softened.
   - Add minced garlic and cook for another minute.
2. **Add Chickpeas and Broth:**
   - Add chickpeas, vegetable broth, and diced tomatoes.
   - Bring to a boil, then reduce heat and simmer for 20 minutes.
3. **Add Spinach and Seasonings:**
   - Stir in fresh spinach, cumin, paprika, salt, black pepper, and lemon juice.
   - Simmer for an additional 5 minutes until spinach is wilted.
4. **Serve:**
   - Garnish with fresh parsley, a dollop of Greek yogurt, and optional red pepper flakes.
   - Serve immediately.

3. Lentil and Vegetable Stew

🔔 Yield: 4 servings   ✂️ Prepration time: 10 Minutes   🍳 Cooking Time: 40 Minutes

Nutritional Information (Per Serving):
- **Calories:** 220
- **Protein:** 10g
- **Carbohydrates:** 35g
- **Fats:** 7g
- **Fiber:** 8g
- **Cholesterol:** 0mg
- **Sodium:** 350mg
- **Potassium:** 700mg

Ingredients:

- **Olive Oil:** 2 tbsp
- **Onion:** 1, chopped
- **Garlic:** 3 cloves, minced
- **Carrot:** 2, diced
- **Celery:** 2 stalks, diced
- **Lentils:** 1 cup, dried, rinsed
- **Vegetable Broth:** 6 cups, low-sodium
- **Diced Tomatoes:** 1 can (15 oz)
- **Potato:** 1 large, diced
- **Bay Leaf:** 1
- **Thyme:** 1 tsp, dried
- **Salt:** 1/2 tsp
- **Black Pepper:** 1/4 tsp

Customizable Ingredients or Garnishes:
- **Fresh Parsley:** For garnish
- **Red Pepper Flakes:** 1/4 tsp (for a spicy kick)
- **Lemon Zest:** 1 tsp (for added flavor)

Instructions:

1. **Cook the Vegetables:**
   - In a large pot, heat olive oil over medium heat.
   - Add chopped onion, diced carrot, and diced celery. Cook for 5 minutes until softened.
   - Add minced garlic and cook for another minute.
2. **Add Lentils and Broth:**
   - Add lentils, vegetable broth, diced tomatoes, diced potato, bay leaf, and dried thyme.
   - Bring to a boil, then reduce heat and simmer for 30-35 minutes until lentils and vegetables are tender.
3. **Season the Stew:**
   - Remove the bay leaf.
   - Stir in salt and black pepper.
4. **Serve:**
   - Garnish with fresh parsley, lemon zest, and optional red pepper flakes.
   - Serve immediately.

4. Butternut Squash Soup

Yield: 4 servings | Prepration time: 10 Minutes | Cooking Time: 30 Minutes

Nutritional Information (Per Serving):
- **Calories:** 180
- **Protein:** 2g
- **Carbohydrates:** 25g
- **Fats:** 9g
- **Fiber:** 5g
- **Cholesterol:** 0mg
- **Sodium:** 300mg
- **Potassium:** 600mg

Ingredients:

- **Olive Oil:** 2 tbsp
- **Onion:** 1, chopped
- **Garlic:** 3 cloves, minced
- **Butternut Squash:** 1 large, peeled and cubed
- **Carrot:** 1, diced
- **Vegetable Broth:** 4 cups, low-sodium
- **Coconut Milk:** 1/2 cup, light
- **Ground Nutmeg:** 1/4 tsp
- **Salt:** 1/2 tsp
- **Black Pepper:** 1/4 tsp

Customizable Ingredients or Garnishes:
- **Fresh Thyme:** For garnish
- **Pumpkin Seeds:** 2 tbsp (for added crunch)
- **Red Pepper Flakes:** 1/4 tsp (for a spicy kick)

Instructions:

1. **Cook the Vegetables:**
   - In a large pot, heat olive oil over medium heat.
   - Add chopped onion and cook for 5 minutes until softened.
   - Add minced garlic, butternut squash, and diced carrot. Cook for another 5 minutes.
2. **Add Broth and Simmer:**
   - Add vegetable broth and bring to a boil.
   - Reduce heat and simmer for 20 minutes until vegetables are tender.
3. **Blend the Soup:**
   - Using an immersion blender or regular blender, blend the soup until smooth.
   - Return to the pot and stir in coconut milk, ground nutmeg, salt, and black pepper.
   - Simmer for an additional 5 minutes.
4. **Serve:**
   - Garnish with fresh thyme, pumpkin seeds, and optional red pepper flakes.
   - Serve immediately.

5. Classic Minestrone

Yield: 4 servings   Prepration time: 10 Minutes   Cooking Time: 30 Minutes

Ingredients:

- **Olive Oil:** 2 tbsp
- **Onion:** 1, chopped
- **Garlic:** 3 cloves, minced
- **Carrot:** 2, diced
- **Celery:** 2 stalks, diced
- **Zucchini:** 1, diced
- **Green Beans:** 1 cup, trimmed and cut into 1-inch pieces
- **Diced Tomatoes:** 1 can (15 oz)
- **Vegetable Broth:** 6 cups, low-sodium
- **Cannellini Beans:** 1 can (15 oz), drained and rinsed
- **Pasta:** 1 cup, whole wheat
  (small shapes like ditalini or elbows)
- **Italian Seasoning:** 1 tsp
- **Salt:** 1/2 tsp
- **Black Pepper:** 1/4 tsp

Nutritional Information (Per Serving):
- Calories: 250
- Protein: 8g
- Carbohydrates: 40g
- Fats: 7g
- Fiber: 8g
- Cholesterol: 0mg
- Sodium: 350mg
- Potassium: 700mg

Customizable Ingredients or Garnishes:
- **Fresh Basil:** For garnish
- **Parmesan Cheese:** 1/4 cup, grated (optional)
- **Red Pepper Flakes:** 1/4 tsp (for a spicy kick)

Instructions:

1. **Cook the Vegetables:**
   - In a large pot, heat olive oil over medium heat.
   - Add chopped onion, diced carrot, and diced celery. Cook for 5 minutes until softened.
   - Add minced garlic and cook for another minute.
2. **Add Broth and Vegetables:**
   - Add diced zucchini, green beans, diced tomatoes, and vegetable broth.
   - Bring to a boil, then reduce heat and simmer for 15 minutes.
3. **Add Beans and Pasta:**
   - Stir in cannellini beans, pasta, Italian seasoning, salt, and black pepper.
   - Cook for an additional 10 minutes until pasta is tender.
4. **Serve:**
   - Garnish with fresh basil, Parmesan cheese, and optional red pepper flakes.
   - Serve immediately.

6. Roasted Red Pepper and Tomato Soup

Yield: 4 servings Prepration time: 10 Minutes Cooking Time: 30 Minutes

Nutritional Information (Per Serving):
- Calories: 130
- Protein: 3g
- Carbohydrates: 18g
- Fats: 7g
- Fiber: 4g
- Cholesterol: 0mg
- Sodium: 250mg
- Potassium: 500mg

Ingredients:

- **Olive Oil:** 2 tbsp
- **Onion:** 1, chopped
- **Garlic:** 3 cloves, minced
- **Roasted Red Peppers:** 2 cups, jarred or homemade, chopped
- **Tomatoes:** 4 large, chopped (or 1 can of diced tomatoes, 28 oz)
- **Vegetable Broth:** 4 cups, low-sodium
- **Tomato Paste:** 2 tbsp
- **Basil:** 1/4 cup, fresh, chopped
- **Salt:** 1/2 tsp
- **Black Pepper:** 1/4 tsp
- **Balsamic Vinegar:** 1 tbsp (optional, for added depth of flavor)

Customizable Ingredients or Garnishes:
- **Fresh Basil Leaves:** For garnish
- **Greek Yogurt:** 1/4 cup, low-fat (for a creamy texture)
- **Red Pepper Flakes:** 1/4 tsp (for a spicy kick)

Instructions:

1. **Cook the Vegetables:**
   - In a large pot, heat olive oil over medium heat.
   - Add chopped onion and cook for 5 minutes until softened.
   - Add minced garlic and cook for another minute.
2. **Add Peppers and Tomatoes:**
   - Add roasted red peppers, chopped tomatoes (or canned tomatoes), vegetable broth, and tomato paste.
   - Bring to a boil, then reduce heat and simmer for 20 minutes.
3. **Blend the Soup:**
   - Using an immersion blender or regular blender, blend the soup until smooth.
   - Return to the pot and stir in fresh basil, salt, black pepper, and optional balsamic vinegar.
   - Simmer for an additional 5 minutes.
4. **Serve:**
   - Garnish with fresh basil leaves, a dollop of Greek yogurt, and optional red pepper flakes.
   - Serve immediately.

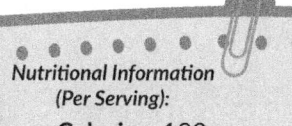

7. Cauliflower and Leek Soup

Yield: 4 servings Prepration time: 10 Minutes Cooking Time: 30 Minutes

Nutritional Information (Per Serving):
- Calories: 160
- Protein: 3g
- Carbohydrates: 15g
- Fats: 9g
- Fiber: 4g
- Cholesterol: 0mg
- Sodium: 250mg
- Potassium: 450mg

Ingredients:

- **Olive Oil:** 2 tbsp
- **Leeks:** 2, white and light green parts only, chopped
- **Garlic:** 3 cloves, minced
- **Cauliflower:** 1 large head, chopped
- **Vegetable Broth:** 4 cups, low-sodium
- **Thyme:** 1 tsp, dried
- **Bay Leaf:** 1
- **Salt:** 1/2 tsp
- **Black Pepper:** 1/4 tsp
- **Coconut Milk:** 1/2 cup, light

Customizable Ingredients or Garnishes:
- **Fresh Chives:** For garnish
- **Pumpkin Seeds:** 2 tbsp (for added crunch)
- **Red Pepper Flakes:** 1/4 tsp (for a spicy kick)

Instructions:

1. **Cook the Vegetables:**
   - In a large pot, heat olive oil over medium heat.
   - Add chopped leeks and cook for 5 minutes until softened.
   - Add minced garlic and cook for another minute.
2. **Add Cauliflower and Broth:**
   - Add chopped cauliflower, vegetable broth, dried thyme, and bay leaf.
   - Bring to a boil, then reduce heat and simmer for 20 minutes until cauliflower is tender.
3. **Blend the Soup:**
   - Remove the bay leaf.
   - Using an immersion blender or regular blender, blend the soup until smooth.
   - Return to the pot and stir in coconut milk, salt, and black pepper.
   - Simmer for an additional 5 minutes.
4. **Serve:**
   - Garnish with fresh chives, pumpkin seeds, and optional red pepper flakes.
   - Serve immediately.

8. Wild Rice and Mushroom Soup

Yield: 4 servings **Prepration time:** 10 Minutes **Cooking Time:** 45 Minutes

Nutritional Information (Per Serving):
- **Calories:** 200
- **Protein:** 5g
- **Carbohydrates:** 28g
- **Fats:** 8g
- **Fiber:** 4g
- **Cholesterol:** 0mg
- **Sodium:** 250mg
- **Potassium:** 500mg

Ingredients:

- **Olive Oil:** 2 tbsp
- **Onion:** 1, chopped
- **Garlic:** 3 cloves, minced
- **Carrot:** 2, diced
- **Celery:** 2 stalks, diced
- **Mushrooms:** 2 cups, sliced
- **Wild Rice:** 1/2 cup, uncooked
- **Vegetable Broth:** 6 cups, low-sodium
- **Thyme:** 1 tsp, dried
- **Bay Leaf:** 1
- **Salt:** 1/2 tsp
- **Black Pepper:** 1/4 tsp
- **Coconut Milk:** 1/2 cup, light

Customizable Ingredients or Garnishes:
- **Fresh Parsley:** For garnish
- **Red Pepper Flakes:** 1/4 tsp (for a spicy kick)

Instructions:

1. **Cook the Vegetables:**
   - In a large pot, heat olive oil over medium heat.
   - Add chopped onion, diced carrot, and diced celery. Cook for 5 minutes until softened.
   - Add minced garlic and cook for another minute.
2. **Add Mushrooms and Rice:**
   - Add sliced mushrooms and cook for 5 minutes until they release their moisture.
   - Add wild rice, vegetable broth, dried thyme, and bay leaf.
   - Bring to a boil, then reduce heat and simmer for 35-40 minutes until rice is tender.
3. **Finish the Soup:**
   - Remove the bay leaf.
   - Stir in coconut milk, salt, and black pepper.
   - Simmer for an additional 5 minutes.
4. **Serve:**
   - Garnish with fresh parsley and optional red pepper flakes.
   - Serve immediately.

9. Carrot Ginger Soup

Yield: 4 servings Prepration time: 10 Minutes Cooking Time: 25 Minutes

Ingredients:

- **Olive Oil:** 2 tbsp
- **Onion:** 1, chopped
- **Garlic:** 3 cloves, minced
- **Carrots:** 6 large, peeled and chopped
- **Ginger:** 1 tbsp, minced
- **Vegetable Broth:** 4 cups, low-sodium
- **Coconut Milk:** 1/2 cup, light
- **Salt:** 1/2 tsp
- **Black Pepper:** 1/4 tsp

Customizable Ingredients or Garnishes:
- **Fresh Cilantro:** For garnish
- **Pumpkin Seeds:** 2 tbsp (for added crunch)
- **Red Pepper Flakes:** 1/4 tsp (for a spicy kick)

Nutritional Information (Per Serving):
- **Calories:** 150
- **Protein:** 2g
- **Carbohydrates:** 20g
- **Fats:** 8g
- **Fiber:** 4g
- **Cholesterol:** 0mg
- **Sodium:** 250mg
- **Potassium:** 500mg

Instructions:

1. **Cook the Vegetables:**
   - In a large pot, heat olive oil over medium heat.
   - Add chopped onion and cook for 5 minutes until softened.
   - Add minced garlic, chopped carrots, and minced ginger. Cook for another 5 minutes.
2. **Add Broth and Simmer:**
   - Add vegetable broth and bring to a boil.
   - Reduce heat and simmer for 15-20 minutes until carrots are tender.
3. **Blend the Soup:**
   - Using an immersion blender or regular blender, blend the soup until smooth.
   - Return to the pot and stir in coconut milk, salt, and black pepper.
   - Simmer for an additional 5 minutes.
4. **Serve:**
   - Garnish with fresh cilantro, pumpkin seeds, and optional red pepper flakes.
   - Serve immediately.

10. Sweet Potato and Black Bean Soup

Yield: 4 servings Prepration time: 10 Minutes Cooking Time: 30 Minutes

Ingredients:

- **Olive Oil:** 2 tbsp
- **Onion:** 1, chopped
- **Garlic:** 3 cloves, minced
- **Sweet Potatoes:** 2 large, peeled and diced
- **Carrot:** 1, diced
- **Celery:** 2 stalks, diced
- **Black Beans:** 1 can (15 oz), drained and rinsed
- **Diced Tomatoes:** 1 can (15 oz)
- **Vegetable Broth:** 4 cups, low-sodium
- **Cumin:** 1 tsp
- **Chili Powder:** 1 tsp
- **Paprika:** 1 tsp
- **Salt:** 1/2 tsp
- **Black Pepper:** 1/4 tsp
- **Lime Juice:** 1 tbsp
- **Fresh Cilantro:** For garnish

Nutritional Information (Per Serving):
- **Calories:** 250
- **Protein:** 6g
- **Carbohydrates:** 40g
- **Fats:** 7g
- **Fiber:** 10g
- **Cholesterol:** 0mg
- **Sodium:** 350mg
- **Potassium:** 700mg

Customizable Ingredients or Garnishes:
- **Avocado:** 1, diced
- **Greek Yogurt:** 1/4 cup, low-fat (for a creamy topping)
- **Red Pepper Flakes:** 1/4 tsp (for a spicy kick)

Instructions:

1. **Cook the Vegetables:**
   - In a large pot, heat olive oil over medium heat.
   - Add chopped onion, diced carrot, and diced celery. Cook for 5 minutes until softened.
   - Add minced garlic and cook for another minute.
2. **Add Sweet Potatoes and Broth:**
   - Add diced sweet potatoes, black beans, diced tomatoes, and vegetable broth.
   - Stir in cumin, chili powder, paprika, salt, and black pepper.
   - Bring to a boil, then reduce heat and simmer for 20 minutes until sweet potatoes are tender.
3. **Finish the Soup:**
   - Stir in lime juice and adjust seasoning if needed.
4. **Serve:**
   - Garnish with fresh cilantro, diced avocado, Greek yogurt, and optional red pepper flakes.
   - Serve immediately.

CHAPTER 7. SALADS

1. Mediterranean Quinoa Salad

Yield: 4 servings **Prepration time:** 15 Minutes **Cooking Time:** 15 Minutes

Nutritional Information (Per Serving):
- **Calories:** 220
- **Protein:** 6g
- **Carbohydrates:** 30g
- **Fats:** 9g
- **Fiber:** 5g
- **Cholesterol:** 0mg
- **Sodium:** 250mg
- **Potassium:** 450mg

Ingredients:

- **Quinoa:** 1 cup, uncooked
- **Water:** 2 cups
- **Cucumber:** 1, diced
- **Cherry Tomatoes:** 1 cup, halved
- **Red Onion:** 1/4 cup, finely chopped
- **Kalamata Olives:** 1/4 cup, sliced
- **Red Bell Pepper:** 1, diced
- **Fresh Parsley:** 1/4 cup, chopped
- **Olive Oil:** 2 tbsp
- **Lemon Juice:** 2 tbsp
- **Salt:** 1/2 tsp
- **Black Pepper:** 1/4 tsp

Customizable Ingredients or Garnishes:
- **Feta Cheese:** 1/4 cup, crumbled (optional)
- **Red Pepper Flakes:** 1/4 tsp (for a spicy kick)
- **Fresh Mint:** 2 tbsp, chopped (for added freshness)

Instructions:

1. **Cook the Quinoa:**
   - Rinse the quinoa under cold water.
   - In a medium pot, bring water to a boil.
   - Add quinoa, reduce heat to low, cover, and simmer for 15 minutes, or until the water is absorbed.
   - Fluff with a fork and let cool.
2. **Prepare the Salad:**
   - In a large bowl, combine cooked quinoa, diced cucumber, halved cherry tomatoes, finely chopped red onion, sliced Kalamata olives, diced red bell pepper, and chopped parsley.
3. **Make the Dressing:**
   - In a small bowl, whisk together olive oil, lemon juice, salt, and black pepper.
4. **Assemble the Salad:**
   - Pour the dressing over the quinoa mixture and toss to combine.
5. **Serve:**
   - Garnish with optional feta cheese, red pepper flakes, and fresh mint.
   - Serve immediately or refrigerate until ready to serve.

2. Chicken and Avocado Salad

Yield: 4 servings **Prepration time:** 15 Minutes **Cooking Time:** 0 Minutes

Nutritional Information (Per Serving):
- **Calories:** 290
- **Protein:** 18g
- **Carbohydrates:** 12g
- **Fats:** 20g
- **Fiber:** 7g
- **Cholesterol:** 50mg
- **Sodium:** 300mg
- **Potassium:** 750mg

Ingredients:

- **Cooked Chicken Breast:** 2 cups, shredded
- **Avocado:** 2, diced
- **Cherry Tomatoes:** 1 cup, halved
- **Cucumber:** 1, diced
- **Red Onion:** 1/4 cup, finely chopped
- **Lime Juice:** 2 tbsp
- **Olive Oil:** 2 tbsp
- **Salt:** 1/2 tsp
- **Black Pepper:** 1/4 tsp
- **Fresh Cilantro:** 1/4 cup, chopped

Customizable Ingredients or Garnishes:
- **Red Pepper Flakes:** 1/4 tsp (for a spicy kick)
- **Feta Cheese:** 1/4 cup, crumbled (optional)
- **Greek Yogurt:** 1/4 cup, low-fat (for added creaminess)

Instructions:

1. **Prepare the Salad:**
   - In a large bowl, combine shredded cooked chicken breast, diced avocado, halved cherry tomatoes, diced cucumber, and finely chopped red onion.
2. **Make the Dressing:**
   - In a small bowl, whisk together lime juice, olive oil, salt, and black pepper.
3. **Assemble the Salad:**
   - Pour the dressing over the chicken mixture and toss to combine.
   - Stir in fresh cilantro.
4. **Serve:**
   - Garnish with optional red pepper flakes, feta cheese, and Greek yogurt.
   - Serve immediately or refrigerate until ready to serve.

3. Kale and Apple Slaw

Yield: 4 servings   Prepration time: 15 Minutes   Cooking Time: 0 Minutes

Ingredients:

- **Kale:** 4 cups, finely chopped
- **Apple:** 1 large, julienned
- **Carrot:** 1 large, grated
- **Red Cabbage:** 1 cup, shredded
- **Green Onion:** 1/4 cup, sliced
- **Olive Oil:** 2 tbsp
- **Apple Cider Vinegar:** 2 tbsp
- **Honey:** 1 tbsp
- **Dijon Mustard:** 1 tsp
- **Salt:** 1/2 tsp
- **Black Pepper:** 1/4 tsp

Nutritional Information (Per Serving):
- Calories: 150
- Protein: 3g
- Carbohydrates: 20g
- Fats: 8g
- Fiber: 5g
- Cholesterol: 0mg
- Sodium: 250mg
- Potassium: 400mg

Customizable Ingredients or Garnishes:
- **Pumpkin Seeds:** 2 tbsp (for added crunch)
- **Dried Cranberries:** 1/4 cup (for a touch of sweetness)
- **Greek Yogurt:** 1/4 cup, low-fat (for added creaminess)

Instructions:

1. **Prepare the Salad:**
   - In a large bowl, combine finely chopped kale, julienned apple, grated carrot, shredded red cabbage, and sliced green onion.
2. **Make the Dressing:**
   - In a small bowl, whisk together olive oil, apple cider vinegar, honey, Dijon mustard, salt, and black pepper.
3. **Assemble the Salad:**
   - Pour the dressing over the kale mixture and toss to combine.
4. **Serve:**
   - Garnish with optional pumpkin seeds, dried cranberries, and Greek yogurt.
   - Serve immediately or refrigerate until ready to serve.

4. Thai-Inspired Shrimp Salad

Yield: 4 servings Prepration time: 15 Minutes Cooking Time: 5 Minutes

Ingredients:

- **Shrimp:** 1 lb, peeled and deveined
- **Olive Oil:** 2 tbsp
- **Garlic:** 2 cloves, minced
- **Lime Juice:** 2 tbsp
- **Fish Sauce:** 1 tbsp
- **Honey:** 1 tbsp
- **Red Chili:** 1, thinly sliced
- **Cucumber:** 1, julienned
- **Carrot:** 1, julienned
- **Red Bell Pepper:** 1, thinly sliced
- **Green Onion:** 1/4 cup, sliced
- **Fresh Cilantro:** 1/4 cup, chopped
- **Fresh Mint:** 1/4 cup, chopped

Nutritional Information (Per Serving):
- **Calories:** 250
- **Protein:** 25g
- **Carbohydrates:** 15g
- **Fats:** 10g
- **Fiber:** 4g
- **Cholesterol:** 200mg
- **Sodium:** 500mg
- **Potassium:** 600mg

Customizable Ingredients or Garnishes:
- **Crushed Peanuts:** 2 tbsp (for added crunch)
- **Avocado:** 1, diced
- **Red Pepper Flakes:** 1/4 tsp (for a spicy kick)

Instructions:

1. **Cook the Shrimp:**
   - In a large skillet, heat olive oil over medium heat.
   - Add minced garlic and cook for 30 seconds until fragrant.
   - Add shrimp and cook for 2-3 minutes on each side until pink and cooked through.
   - Remove from heat and let cool.
2. **Prepare the Salad:**
   - In a large bowl, combine julienned cucumber, julienned carrot, thinly sliced red bell pepper, and sliced green onion.
3. **Make the Dressing:**
   - In a small bowl, whisk together lime juice, fish sauce, honey, and thinly sliced red chili.
4. **Assemble the Salad:**
   - Add the cooked shrimp to the vegetable mixture.
   - Pour the dressing over the salad and toss to combine.
   - Stir in fresh cilantro and mint.
5. **Serve:**
   - Garnish with optional crushed peanuts, diced avocado, and red pepper flakes.
   - Serve immediately.

5. Greek Salad with Low-Fat Feta

🍽 Yield: 4 servings ⏱ Prepration time: 15 Minutes 👨‍🍳 Cooking Time: 0 Minutes

Ingredients:

- **Cucumber:** 1, diced
- **Cherry Tomatoes:** 1 cup, halved
- **Red Onion:** 1/4 cup, thinly sliced
- **Kalamata Olives:** 1/4 cup, halved
- **Green Bell Pepper:** 1, diced
- **Low-Fat Feta Cheese:** 1/2 cup, crumbled
- **Olive Oil:** 2 tbsp
- **Red Wine Vinegar:** 2 tbsp
- **Oregano:** 1 tsp, dried
- **Salt:** 1/2 tsp
- **Black Pepper:** 1/4 tsp

Nutritional Information (Per Serving):
- **Calories:** 180
- **Protein:** 6g
- **Carbohydrates:** 10g
- **Fats:** 14g
- **Fiber:** 3g
- **Cholesterol:** 15mg
- **Sodium:** 400mg
- **Potassium:** 350mg

Customizable Ingredients or Garnishes:
- **Fresh Dill:** 2 tbsp, chopped (for added flavor)
- **Red Pepper Flakes:** 1/4 tsp (for a spicy kick)
- **Avocado:** 1, diced (for added creaminess)

Instructions:

1. **Prepare the Salad:**
   - In a large bowl, combine diced cucumber, halved cherry tomatoes, thinly sliced red onion, halved Kalamata olives, diced green bell pepper, and crumbled low-fat feta cheese.
2. **Make the Dressing:**
   - In a small bowl, whisk together olive oil, red wine vinegar, oregano, salt, and black pepper.
3. **Assemble the Salad:**
   - Pour the dressing over the vegetable mixture and toss to combine.
4. **Serve:**
   - Garnish with fresh dill, red pepper flakes, and optional diced avocado.
   - Serve immediately or refrigerate until ready to serve.

6. Spinach and Strawberry Salad

Yield: 4 servings Prepration time: 10 Minutes Cooking Time: 0 Minutes

Nutritional Information (Per Serving):
- Calories: 140
- Protein: 3g
- Carbohydrates: 12g
- Fats: 10g
- Fiber: 3g
- Cholesterol: 0mg
- Sodium: 150mg
- Potassium: 400mg

Ingredients:

- **Baby Spinach:** 4 cups
- **Strawberries:** 1 cup, sliced
- **Red Onion:** 1/4 cup, thinly sliced
- **Almonds:** 1/4 cup, sliced
- **Feta Cheese:** 1/4 cup, crumbled (optional)
- **Olive Oil:** 2 tbsp
- **Balsamic Vinegar:** 2 tbsp
- **Honey:** 1 tbsp
- **Salt:** 1/4 tsp
- **Black Pepper:** 1/4 tsp

Customizable Ingredients or Garnishes:
- **Avocado:** 1, diced
- **Poppy Seeds:** 1 tsp (for added texture)
- **Red Pepper Flakes:** 1/4 tsp (for a spicy kick)

Instructions:

1. **Prepare the Salad:**
   - In a large bowl, combine baby spinach, sliced strawberries, thinly sliced red onion, and sliced almonds.
2. **Make the Dressing:**
   - In a small bowl, whisk together olive oil, balsamic vinegar, honey, salt, and black pepper.
3. **Assemble the Salad:**
   - Pour the dressing over the spinach mixture and toss to combine.
4. **Serve:**
   - Garnish with optional feta cheese, diced avocado, poppy seeds, and red pepper flakes.
   - Serve immediately.

7. Black Bean and Corn Salad

Yield: 4 servings *Prepration time: 15 Minutes* *Cooking Time: 0 Minutes*

Ingredients:

- **Black Beans:** 1 can (15 oz), drained and rinsed
- **Corn Kernels:** 1 cup, cooked (fresh or frozen)
- **Red Bell Pepper:** 1, diced
- **Red Onion:** 1/4 cup, finely chopped
- **Cherry Tomatoes:** 1 cup, halved
- **Cilantro:** 1/4 cup, chopped
- **Olive Oil:** 2 tbsp
- **Lime Juice:** 2 tbsp
- **Cumin:** 1 tsp
- **Salt:** 1/2 tsp
- **Black Pepper:** 1/4 tsp

Customizable Ingredients or Garnishes:

- **Avocado:** 1, diced
- **Feta Cheese:** 1/4 cup, crumbled (optional)
- **Red Pepper Flakes:** 1/4 tsp (for a spicy kick)

Nutritional Information (Per Serving):

- **Calories:** 180
- **Protein:** 6g
- **Carbohydrates:** 25g
- **Fats:** 7g
- **Fiber:** 7g
- **Cholesterol:** 0mg
- **Sodium:** 300mg
- **Potassium:** 500mg

Instructions:

1. **Prepare the Salad:**
   - In a large bowl, combine black beans, cooked corn kernels, diced red bell pepper, finely chopped red onion, halved cherry tomatoes, and chopped cilantro.
2. **Make the Dressing:**
   - In a small bowl, whisk together olive oil, lime juice, cumin, salt, and black pepper.
3. **Assemble the Salad:**
   - Pour the dressing over the bean mixture and toss to combine.
4. **Serve:**
   - Garnish with optional diced avocado, feta cheese, and red pepper flakes.
   - Serve immediately or refrigerate until ready to serve.

8. Arugula and Beet Salad

Yield: 4 servings *Prepration time: 10 Minutes* *Cooking Time: 40 Minutes*

Ingredients:

- **Beets:** 4 small, roasted and sliced
- **Arugula:** 4 cups
- **Goat Cheese:** 1/4 cup, crumbled (optional)
- **Walnuts:** 1/4 cup, toasted
- **Olive Oil:** 2 tbsp
- **Balsamic Vinegar:** 2 tbsp
- **Honey:** 1 tbsp
- **Salt:** 1/4 tsp
- **Black Pepper:** 1/4 tsp

Customizable Ingredients or Garnishes:
- **Orange Segments:** 1 cup (for added sweetness)
- **Avocado:** 1, diced (for added creaminess)
- **Red Pepper Flakes:** 1/4 tsp (for a spicy kick)

Nutritional Information (Per Serving):
- **Calories:** 200
- **Protein:** 5g
- **Carbohydrates:** 20g
- **Fats:** 12g
- **Fiber:** 5g
- **Cholesterol:** 5mg
- **Sodium:** 250mg
- **Potassium:** 600mg

Instructions:

1. **Roast the Beets:**
   - Preheat the oven to 400°F (200°C).
   - Wrap the beets in aluminum foil and roast for 40 minutes or until tender.
   - Let cool, then peel and slice.
2. **Prepare the Salad:**
   - In a large bowl, combine arugula, sliced roasted beets, crumbled goat cheese, and toasted walnuts.
3. **Make the Dressing:**
   - In a small bowl, whisk together olive oil, balsamic vinegar, honey, salt, and black pepper.
4. **Assemble the Salad:**
   - Pour the dressing over the arugula mixture and toss to combine.
5. **Serve:**
   - Garnish with optional orange segments, diced avocado, and red pepper flakes.
   - Serve immediately.

9. Cucumber and Dill Salad

Yield: 4 servings Prepration time: 10 Minutes Cooking Time: 0 Minutes

Ingredients:

- **Cucumber:** 2 large, thinly sliced
- **Red Onion:** 1/4 cup, thinly sliced
- **Greek Yogurt:** 1/2 cup, low-fat
- **Fresh Dill:** 2 tbsp, chopped
- **Lemon Juice:** 1 tbsp
- **Salt:** 1/2 tsp
- **Black Pepper:** 1/4 tsp

Customizable Ingredients or Garnishes:
- **Avocado:** 1, diced (for added creaminess)
- **Cherry Tomatoes:** 1 cup, halved (for added color)
- **Red Pepper Flakes:** 1/4 tsp (for a spicy kick)

Nutritional Information (Per Serving):
- **Calories:** 60
- **Protein:** 3g
- **Carbohydrates:** 10g
- **Fats:** 2g
- **Fiber:** 2g
- **Cholesterol:** 0mg
- **Sodium:** 250mg
- **Potassium:** 350mg

Instructions:

1. **Prepare the Salad:**
   - In a large bowl, combine thinly sliced cucumber and red onion.
2. **Make the Dressing:**
   - In a small bowl, whisk together Greek yogurt, fresh dill, lemon juice, salt, and black pepper.
3. **Assemble the Salad:**
   - Pour the dressing over the cucumber mixture and toss to combine.
4. **Serve:**
   - Garnish with optional diced avocado, cherry tomatoes, and red pepper flakes.
   - Serve immediately or refrigerate until ready to serve.

10. Mixed Greens with Berries and Walnuts

Yield: 4 servings | Prepration time: 10 Minutes | Cooking Time: 0 Minutes

Nutritional Information (Per Serving):
- Calories: 160
- Protein: 3g
- Carbohydrates: 15g
- Fats: 10g
- Fiber: 4g
- Cholesterol: 0mg
- Sodium: 150mg
- Potassium: 350mg

Ingredients:

- **Mixed Greens:** 4 cups
- **Strawberries:** 1 cup, sliced
- **Blueberries:** 1/2 cup
- **Walnuts:** 1/4 cup, toasted
- **Feta Cheese:** 1/4 cup, crumbled (optional)
- **Olive Oil:** 2 tbsp
- **Balsamic Vinegar:** 2 tbsp
- **Honey:** 1 tbsp
- **Salt:** 1/4 tsp
- **Black Pepper:** 1/4 tsp

Customizable Ingredients or Garnishes:
- **Avocado:** 1, diced (for added creaminess)
- **Poppy Seeds:** 1 tsp (for added texture)
- **Red Pepper Flakes:** 1/4 tsp (for a spicy kick)

Instructions:

1. **Prepare the Salad:**
   - In a large bowl, combine mixed greens, sliced strawberries, blueberries, and toasted walnuts.
2. **Make the Dressing:**
   - In a small bowl, whisk together olive oil, balsamic vinegar, honey, salt, and black pepper.
3. **Assemble the Salad:**
   - Pour the dressing over the greens mixture and toss to combine.
4. **Serve:**
   - Garnish with optional feta cheese, diced avocado, poppy seeds, and red pepper flakes.
   - Serve immediately.

CHAPTER 8. VEGETARIAN MAINS

1. Stuffed Bell Peppers with Quinoa and Black Beans

Yield: 4 servings Prepration time: 15 Minutes Cooking Time: 30 Minutes

Nutritional Information (Per Serving):
- **Calories:** 200
- **Protein:** 7g
- **Carbohydrates:** 35g
- **Fats:** 6g
- **Fiber:** 8g
- **Cholesterol:** 0mg
- **Sodium:** 350mg
- **Potassium:** 700mg

Ingredients:

- **Bell Peppers:** 4 large, tops cut off and seeds removed
- **Quinoa:** 1 cup, cooked
- **Black Beans:** 1 can (15 oz), drained and rinsed
- **Corn Kernels:** 1 cup, cooked
- **Tomato:** 1, diced
- **Onion:** 1/4 cup, finely chopped
- **Cumin:** 1 tsp
- **Chili Powder:** 1 tsp
- **Salt:** 1/2 tsp
- **Black Pepper:** 1/4 tsp
- **Olive Oil:** 1 tbsp
- **Fresh Cilantro:** 2 tbsp, chopped

Customizable Ingredients or Garnishes:
- **Cheddar Cheese:** 1/4 cup, shredded (optional)
- **Avocado:** 1, diced (for serving)
- **Salsa:** 1/2 cup (for serving)

Instructions:

1. **Preheat the Oven:**
   - Preheat the oven to 375°F (190°C).
2. **Prepare the Filling:**
   - In a large bowl, combine cooked quinoa, black beans, corn, diced tomato, finely chopped onion, cumin, chili powder, salt, and black pepper.
   - Mix until well combined.
3. **Stuff the Peppers:**
   - Spoon the filling into the bell peppers.
4. **Bake the Peppers:**
   - Place the stuffed peppers in a baking dish.
   - Drizzle with olive oil.
   - Bake for 25-30 minutes, or until the peppers are tender.
5. **Serve:**
   - Garnish with fresh cilantro and optional cheddar cheese.
   - Serve with diced avocado and salsa.

2. Spaghetti Squash with Marinara Sauce

Yield: 4 servings *Prepration time: 10 Minutes* *Cooking Time: 40 Minutes*

Ingredients:

- **Spaghetti Squash:** 1 large
- **Olive Oil:** 2 tbsp
- **Marinara Sauce:** 2 cups, low-sodium
- **Garlic:** 2 cloves, minced
- **Salt:** 1/2 tsp
- **Black Pepper:** 1/4 tsp
- **Fresh Basil:** 1/4 cup, chopped
- **Parmesan Cheese:** 1/4 cup, grated (optional)

Customizable Ingredients or Garnishes:
- **Red Pepper Flakes:** 1/4 tsp (for a spicy kick)
- **Fresh Parsley:** 2 tbsp, chopped (for garnish)

Nutritional Information (Per Serving):
- **Calories:** 150
- **Protein:** 3g
- **Carbohydrates:** 18g
- **Fats:** 8g
- **Fiber:** 4g
- **Cholesterol:** 0mg
- **Sodium:** 300mg
- **Potassium:** 500mg

Instructions:

1. **Preheat the Oven:**
   - Preheat the oven to 400°F (200°C).
2. **Prepare the Spaghetti Squash:**
   - Cut the spaghetti squash in half lengthwise and remove the seeds.
   - Drizzle with olive oil and season with salt and black pepper.
   - Place the squash halves cut-side down on a baking sheet.
   - Bake for 35-40 minutes, or until the squash is tender.
3. **Make the Marinara Sauce:**
   - In a large saucepan, heat olive oil over medium heat.
   - Add minced garlic and cook for 1 minute until fragrant.
   - Add marinara sauce and simmer for 10 minutes.
4. **Scrape the Squash:**
   - Use a fork to scrape the flesh of the cooked squash into spaghetti-like strands.
5. **Serve:**
   - Top the spaghetti squash strands with marinara sauce.
   - Garnish with fresh basil, Parmesan cheese, and optional red pepper flakes and parsley.
   - Serve immediately.

3. Chickpea and Vegetable Curry

🔔 Yield: 4 servings ✂️ Prepration time: 15 Minutes 🍳 Cooking Time: 30 Minutes

Nutritional Information (Per Serving):
- **Calories:** 250
- **Protein:** 6g
- **Carbohydrates:** 30g
- **Fats:** 12g
- **Fiber:** 8g
- **Cholesterol:** 0mg
- **Sodium:** 350mg
- **Potassium:** 700mg

Ingredients:

- **Olive Oil:** 2 tbsp
- **Onion:** 1, chopped
- **Garlic:** 3 cloves, minced
- **Ginger:** 1 tbsp, minced
- **Carrot:** 2, diced
- **Bell Pepper:** 1, diced
- **Zucchini:** 1, diced
- **Chickpeas:** 1 can (15 oz), drained and rinsed
- **Coconut Milk:** 1 can (15 oz), light
- **Diced Tomatoes:** 1 can (15 oz)
- **Curry Powder:** 2 tbsp
- **Cumin:** 1 tsp
- **Coriander:** 1 tsp
- **Salt:** 1/2 tsp
- **Black Pepper:** 1/4 tsp
- **Fresh Cilantro:** 1/4 cup, chopped

Customizable Ingredients or Garnishes:
- **Lime Wedges:** For serving
- **Red Pepper Flakes:** 1/4 tsp (for a spicy kick)
- **Greek Yogurt:** 1/4 cup, low-fat (for added creaminess)

Instructions:

1. **Cook the Vegetables:**
   - In a large pot, heat olive oil over medium heat.
   - Add chopped onion, minced garlic, and minced ginger. Cook for 5 minutes until softened.
   - Add diced carrot, bell pepper, and zucchini. Cook for another 5 minutes.
2. **Add Chickpeas and Spices:**
   - Add chickpeas, curry powder, cumin, coriander, salt, and black pepper. Stir to coat the vegetables and chickpeas with the spices.
3. **Add Coconut Milk and Tomatoes:**
   - Stir in coconut milk and diced tomatoes.
   - Bring to a boil, then reduce heat and simmer for 20 minutes until vegetables are tender.
4. **Serve:**
   - Garnish with fresh cilantro, lime wedges, and optional red pepper flakes and Greek yogurt.
   - Serve immediately.

4. Eggplant Parmesan

Yield: 4 servings   Prepration time: 15 Minutes   Cooking Time: 40 Minutes

Ingredients:

- **Eggplant:** 1 large, sliced into rounds
- **Olive Oil:** 2 tbsp
- **Marinara Sauce:** 2 cups, low-sodium
- **Mozzarella Cheese:** 1 cup, shredded, low-fat
- **Parmesan Cheese:** 1/4 cup, grated
- **Whole Wheat Breadcrumbs:** 1 cup
- **Egg:** 1 large, beaten
- **Garlic Powder:** 1 tsp
- **Dried Oregano:** 1 tsp
- **Salt:** 1/2 tsp
- **Black Pepper:** 1/4 tsp

Nutritional Information (Per Serving):
- **Calories:** 250
- **Protein:** 10g
- **Carbohydrates:** 25g
- **Fats:** 12g
- **Fiber:** 6g
- **Cholesterol:** 50mg
- **Sodium:** 450mg
- **Potassium:** 500mg

Customizable Ingredients or Garnishes:
- **Fresh Basil:** 2 tbsp, chopped (for garnish)
- **Red Pepper Flakes:** 1/4 tsp (for a spicy kick)

Instructions:

1. **Preheat the Oven:**
   - Preheat the oven to 375°F (190°C).
2. **Prepare the Eggplant:**
   - Dip each eggplant slice in the beaten egg, then coat with a mixture of whole wheat breadcrumbs, garlic powder, dried oregano, salt, and black pepper.
3. **Bake the Eggplant:**
   - Place the eggplant slices on a baking sheet lined with parchment paper.
   - Drizzle with olive oil and bake for 20 minutes, flipping halfway through, until golden brown and crispy.
4. **Assemble the Dish:**
   - In a baking dish, spread a layer of marinara sauce.
   - Add a layer of baked eggplant slices, then top with more marinara sauce and shredded mozzarella cheese.
   - Repeat the layers, finishing with a layer of marinara sauce and a sprinkle of Parmesan cheese.
5. **Bake the Dish:**
   - Bake for an additional 20 minutes, until the cheese is melted and bubbly.
6. **Serve:**
   - Garnish with fresh basil and optional red pepper flakes.
   - Serve immediately.

5. Portobello Mushroom Burgers

Yield: 4 servings   *Prepration time: 10 Minutes*   *Cooking Time: 15 Minutes*

Nutritional Information (Per Serving):
- Calories: 220
- Protein: 6g
- Carbohydrates: 30g
- Fats: 10g
- Fiber: 6g
- Cholesterol: 0mg
- Sodium: 400mg
- Potassium: 700mg

Ingredients:

- **Portobello Mushrooms:** 4 large, stems removed
- **Olive Oil:** 2 tbsp
- **Balsamic Vinegar:** 2 tbsp
- **Garlic:** 2 cloves, minced
- **Salt:** 1/2 tsp
- **Black Pepper:** 1/4 tsp
- **Whole Wheat Burger Buns:** 4
- **Tomato:** 1, sliced
- **Lettuce:** 4 leaves
- **Red Onion:** 1/4 cup, thinly sliced

Customizable Ingredients or Garnishes:
- **Avocado:** 1, sliced
- **Feta Cheese:** 1/4 cup, crumbled (optional)
- **Mustard:** 2 tbsp (for added flavor)

Instructions:

1. **Marinate the Mushrooms:**
   - In a small bowl, whisk together olive oil, balsamic vinegar, minced garlic, salt, and black pepper.
   - Brush the mixture onto both sides of the portobello mushrooms.
2. **Cook the Mushrooms:**
   - Preheat a grill or grill pan to medium-high heat.
   - Grill the mushrooms for 5-7 minutes on each side until tender and slightly charred.
3. **Prepare the Buns:**
   - Toast the whole wheat burger buns on the grill for 1-2 minutes until lightly browned.
4. **Assemble the Burgers:**
   - Place a grilled portobello mushroom on each bun.
   - Top with a slice of tomato, a lettuce leaf, thinly sliced red onion, and optional avocado slices and feta cheese.
5. **Serve:**
   - Serve immediately with optional mustard.

6. Sweet Potato and Black Bean Enchiladas

Yield: 4 servings Prepration time: 15 Minutes Cooking Time: 30 Minutes

Ingredients:

- **Sweet Potato:** 2 large, peeled and diced
- **Black Beans:** 1 can (15 oz), drained and rinsed
- **Olive Oil:** 2 tbsp
- **Onion:** 1, chopped
- **Garlic:** 3 cloves, minced
- **Cumin:** 1 tsp
- **Chili Powder:** 1 tsp
- **Salt:** 1/2 tsp
- **Black Pepper:** 1/4 tsp
- **Corn Tortillas:** 8
- **Enchilada Sauce:** 2 cups, low-sodium
- **Cheddar Cheese:** 1/2 cup, shredded, low-fat (optional)
- **Fresh Cilantro:** 1/4 cup, chopped

Customizable Ingredients or Garnishes:
- **Avocado:** 1, diced
- **Greek Yogurt:** 1/4 cup, low-fat (for a creamy topping)
- **Salsa:** 1/2 cup (for serving)

Nutritional Information (Per Serving):
- **Calories:** 300
- **Protein:** 8g
- **Carbohydrates:** 50g
- **Fats:** 10g
- **Fiber:** 10g
- **Cholesterol:** 0mg
- **Sodium:** 400mg
- **Potassium:** 800mg

Instructions:

1. **Preheat the Oven:**
   - Preheat the oven to 375°F (190°C).
2. **Cook the Sweet Potatoes:**
   - In a large pot, bring water to a boil.
   - Add diced sweet potatoes and cook for 10 minutes until tender.
   - Drain and set aside.
3. **Prepare the Filling:**
   - In a large skillet, heat olive oil over medium heat.
   - Add chopped onion and cook for 5 minutes until softened.
   - Add minced garlic, cumin, chili powder, salt, and black beans. Cook for another 5 minutes.
   - Stir in cooked sweet potatoes and mix until well combined.
4. **Assemble the Enchiladas:**
   - Spread 1/2 cup of enchilada sauce on the bottom of a baking dish.
   - Place a few spoonfuls of the sweet potato mixture onto each tortilla, roll them up, and place seam-side down in the baking dish.
   - Pour the remaining enchilada sauce over the top and sprinkle with optional cheddar cheese.
5. **Bake the Enchiladas:**
   - Bake for 20 minutes until the sauce is bubbly and the cheese is melted.
6. **Serve:**
   - Garnish with fresh cilantro, diced avocado, Greek yogurt, and salsa.
   - Serve immediately.

7. Lentil and Spinach Stuffed Acorn Squash

Yield: 4 servings   Prepration time: 15 Minutes   Cooking Time: 45 Minutes

Ingredients:

Nutritional Information (Per Serving):
- Calories: 300
- Protein: 10g
- Carbohydrates: 45g
- Fats: 10g
- Fiber: 12g
- Cholesterol: 0mg
- Sodium: 400mg
- Potassium: 900mg

- **Acorn Squash:** 2 large, halved and seeds removed
- **Olive Oil:** 2 tbsp
- **Onion:** 1, chopped
- **Garlic:** 3 cloves, minced
- **Carrot:** 2, diced
- **Celery:** 2 stalks, diced
- **Lentils:** 1 cup, dried, rinsed
- **Vegetable Broth:** 4 cups, low-sodium
- **Fresh Spinach:** 4 cups, chopped
- **Thyme:** 1 tsp, dried
- **Salt:** 1/2 tsp
- **Black Pepper:** 1/4 tsp
- **Parmesan Cheese:** 1/4 cup, grated (optional)

Customizable Ingredients or Garnishes:
- **Fresh Parsley:** 2 tbsp, chopped (for garnish)
- **Red Pepper Flakes:** 1/4 tsp (for a spicy kick)
- **Greek Yogurt:** 1/4 cup, low-fat (for a creamy topping)

Instructions:

1. **Preheat the Oven:**
   - Preheat the oven to 400°F (200°C).
2. **Roast the Acorn Squash:**
   - Brush the cut sides of the acorn squash with 1 tbsp of olive oil and place cut-side down on a baking sheet.
   - Roast for 30-35 minutes until tender.
3. **Prepare the Filling:**
   - In a large pot, heat 1 tbsp of olive oil over medium heat.
   - Add chopped onion, diced carrot, and diced celery. Cook for 5 minutes until softened.
   - Add minced garlic, lentils, vegetable broth, dried thyme, salt, and black pepper. Bring to a boil, then reduce heat and simmer for 20 minutes until lentils are tender.
   - Stir in chopped spinach and cook for an additional 2-3 minutes until wilted.
4. **Stuff the Squash:**
   - Spoon the lentil and spinach mixture into the roasted acorn squash halves.
5. **Serve:**
   - Garnish with optional Parmesan cheese, fresh parsley, red pepper flakes, and Greek yogurt.
   - Serve immediately.

8. Cauliflower Chickpea Tacos

Yield: 4 servings **Prepration time:** 15 Minutes **Cooking Time:** 30 Minutes

Ingredients:

- **Cauliflower:** 1 medium head, chopped into florets
- **Chickpeas:** 1 can (15 oz), drained and rinsed
- **Olive Oil:** 2 tbsp
- **Cumin:** 1 tsp
- **Chili Powder:** 1 tsp
- **Garlic Powder:** 1 tsp
- **Salt:** 1/2 tsp
- **Black Pepper:** 1/4 tsp
- **Corn Tortillas:** 8
- **Avocado:** 1, sliced
- **Red Cabbage:** 1 cup, shredded
- **Lime:** 1, cut into wedges
- **Fresh Cilantro:** 1/4 cup, chopped

Nutritional Information (Per Serving):
- **Calories:** 300
- **Protein:** 8g
- **Carbohydrates:** 40g
- **Fats:** 12g
- **Fiber:** 10g
- **Cholesterol:** 0mg
- **Sodium:** 400mg
- **Potassium:** 700mg

Customizable Ingredients or Garnishes:
- **Salsa:** 1/2 cup
- **Greek Yogurt:** 1/4 cup, low-fat (for a creamy topping)
- **Red Pepper Flakes:** 1/4 tsp (for a spicy kick)

Instructions:

1. **Preheat the Oven:**
   - Preheat the oven to 400°F (200°C).
2. **Roast the Cauliflower and Chickpeas:**
   - In a large bowl, combine cauliflower florets, chickpeas, olive oil, cumin, chili powder, garlic powder, salt, and black pepper.
   - Spread the mixture on a baking sheet in a single layer.
   - Roast for 25-30 minutes, stirring halfway through, until cauliflower is tender and golden.
3. **Prepare the Toppings:**
   - While the cauliflower and chickpeas are roasting, prepare the avocado slices, shredded red cabbage, lime wedges, and fresh cilantro.
4. **Warm the Tortillas:**
   - Warm the corn tortillas in a dry skillet over medium heat for about 1 minute on each side.
5. **Assemble the Tacos:**
   - Divide the roasted cauliflower and chickpeas among the tortillas.
   - Top with avocado slices, shredded red cabbage, and fresh cilantro.
   - Serve with lime wedges and optional salsa, Greek yogurt, and red pepper flakes.

9. Zucchini Noodles with Pesto

Yield: 4 servings   Prepration time: 15 Minutes   Cooking Time: 5 Minutes

Nutritional Information (Per Serving):
- **Calories:** 200
- **Protein:** 4g
- **Carbohydrates:** 12g
- **Fats:** 16g
- **Fiber:** 4g
- **Cholesterol:** 0mg
- **Sodium:** 300mg
- **Potassium:** 600mg

Ingredients:

- **Zucchini:** 4 large, spiralized into noodles
- **Olive Oil:** 2 tbsp
- **Cherry Tomatoes:** 1 cup, halved
- **Basil Pesto:** 1/2 cup, homemade or store-bought, low-fat
- **Garlic:** 2 cloves, minced
- **Salt:** 1/2 tsp
- **Black Pepper:** 1/4 tsp
- **Pine Nuts:** 2 tbsp, toasted (optional)

Customizable Ingredients or Garnishes:
- **Parmesan Cheese:** 1/4 cup, grated (optional)
- **Red Pepper Flakes:** 1/4 tsp (for a spicy kick)

Instructions:

1. **Prepare the Zucchini Noodles:**
   - Spiralize the zucchinis into noodles using a spiralizer or julienne peeler.
2. **Cook the Noodles:**
   - In a large skillet, heat olive oil over medium heat.
   - Add minced garlic and cook for 1 minute until fragrant.
   - Add zucchini noodles and cook for 2-3 minutes until tender but still crisp.
3. **Add Pesto and Tomatoes:**
   - Remove the skillet from heat.
   - Toss the zucchini noodles with basil pesto and halved cherry tomatoes.
4. **Serve:**
   - Season with salt and black pepper.
   - Garnish with optional toasted pine nuts, Parmesan cheese, and red pepper flakes.
   - Serve immediately.

10. Vegetable Stir-Fry with Tofu

Yield: 4 servings   Prepration time: 15 Minutes   Cooking Time: 15 Minutes

Ingredients:

- **Firm Tofu:** 1 block (14 oz), drained and cubed
- **Olive Oil:** 2 tbsp
- **Broccoli Florets:** 2 cups
- **Bell Pepper:** 1, sliced
- **Carrot:** 1, sliced
- **Snow Peas:** 1 cup
- **Garlic:** 3 cloves, minced
- **Ginger:** 1 tbsp, minced
- **Soy Sauce:** 1/4 cup, low-sodium
- **Sesame Oil:** 1 tsp
- **Cornstarch:** 1 tbsp (optional, for thickening)
- **Water:** 2 tbsp (optional, for thickening)

Nutritional Information (Per Serving):
- Calories: 220
- Protein: 12g
- Carbohydrates: 14g
- Fats: 14g
- Fiber: 4g
- Cholesterol: 0mg
- Sodium: 400mg
- Potassium: 500mg

Customizable Ingredients or Garnishes:
- **Green Onion:** 1/4 cup, sliced (for garnish)
- **Sesame Seeds:** 1 tbsp (for garnish)
- **Red Pepper Flakes:** 1/4 tsp (for a spicy kick)

Instructions:

1. **Prepare the Tofu:**
   - Press the tofu to remove excess moisture, then cut into cubes.
2. **Cook the Tofu:**
   - In a large skillet, heat 1 tbsp of olive oil over medium-high heat.
   - Add tofu cubes and cook until golden brown on all sides, about 5-7 minutes.
   - Remove from the skillet and set aside.
3. **Cook the Vegetables:**
   - In the same skillet, heat the remaining 1 tbsp of olive oil.
   - Add minced garlic and ginger, and cook for 1 minute until fragrant.
   - Add broccoli florets, bell pepper, carrot, and snow peas. Stir-fry for 5-7 minutes until vegetables are tender-crisp.
4. **Combine Tofu and Sauce:**
   - Return the tofu to the skillet.
   - Add soy sauce and sesame oil, stirring to coat.
   - If thickening the sauce, mix cornstarch and water in a small bowl, then add to the skillet and cook until the sauce thickens.
5. **Serve:**
   - Garnish with green onion, sesame seeds, and optional red pepper flakes.
   - Serve immediately.

11. Baked Ratatouille

Yield: 4 servings   *Prepration time: 20 Minutes*   *Cooking Time: 45 Minutes*

Ingredients:

- **Olive Oil:** 3 tbsp
- **Onion:** 1, chopped
- **Garlic:** 3 cloves, minced
- **Eggplant:** 1 large, diced
- **Zucchini:** 2, sliced
- **Bell Pepper:** 1, diced
- **Tomatoes:** 4, diced
- **Tomato Paste:** 2 tbsp
- **Dried Thyme:** 1 tsp
- **Dried Oregano:** 1 tsp
- **Salt:** 1/2 tsp
- **Black Pepper:** 1/4 tsp
- **Fresh Basil:** 1/4 cup, chopped

Nutritional Information (Per Serving):
- **Calories:** 180
- **Protein:** 4g
- **Carbohydrates:** 25g
- **Fats:** 10g
- **Fiber:** 7g
- **Cholesterol:** 0mg
- **Sodium:** 300mg
- **Potassium:** 700mg

Customizable Ingredients or Garnishes:
- **Parmesan Cheese:** 1/4 cup, grated (optional)
- **Red Pepper Flakes:** 1/4 tsp (for a spicy kick)

Instructions:

1. **Preheat the Oven:**
   - Preheat the oven to 375°F (190°C).
2. **Prepare the Vegetables:**
   - In a large oven-safe skillet or Dutch oven, heat olive oil over medium heat.
   - Add chopped onion and minced garlic, and cook for 5 minutes until softened.
   - Add diced eggplant, zucchini, bell pepper, and tomatoes. Cook for another 10 minutes.
3. **Add Seasonings:**
   - Stir in tomato paste, dried thyme, dried oregano, salt, and black pepper.
4. **Bake the Ratatouille:**
   - Transfer the skillet or Dutch oven to the preheated oven.
   - Bake for 30-35 minutes until the vegetables are tender and the flavors have melded.
5. **Serve:**
   - Garnish with fresh basil and optional Parmesan cheese and red pepper flakes.
   - Serve immediately.

12. Quinoa and Vegetable Stuffed Zucchini Boats

Yield: 4 servings   Prepration time: 15 Minutes   Cooking Time: 30 Minutes

Nutritional Information (Per Serving):
- Calories: 250
- Protein: 8g
- Carbohydrates: 35g
- Fats: 10g
- Fiber: 8g
- Cholesterol: 0mg
- Sodium: 350mg
- Potassium: 700mg

Ingredients:

- **Zucchini:** 4 large, halved and seeds removed
- **Quinoa:** 1 cup, cooked
- **Olive Oil:** 2 tbsp
- **Onion:** 1, chopped
- **Garlic:** 2 cloves, minced
- **Tomato:** 1, diced
- **Bell Pepper:** 1, diced
- **Corn Kernels:** 1 cup, cooked
- **Black Beans:** 1 can (15 oz), drained and rinsed
- **Cumin:** 1 tsp
- **Chili Powder:** 1 tsp
- **Salt:** 1/2 tsp
- **Black Pepper:** 1/4 tsp
- **Fresh Cilantro:** 1/4 cup, chopped

Customizable Ingredients or Garnishes:
- **Cheddar Cheese:** 1/4 cup, shredded, low-fat (optional)
- **Avocado:** 1, diced (for serving)
- **Salsa:** 1/2 cup (for serving)

Instructions:

1. **Preheat the Oven:**
   - Preheat the oven to 375°F (190°C).
2. **Prepare the Filling:**
   - In a large skillet, heat olive oil over medium heat.
   - Add chopped onion and cook for 5 minutes until softened.
   - Add minced garlic, diced tomato, bell pepper, corn, black beans, cumin, chili powder, salt, and black pepper. Cook for another 5 minutes.
   - Stir in cooked quinoa.
3. **Stuff the Zucchini:**
   - Spoon the filling into the zucchini halves.
   - Place the stuffed zucchini in a baking dish.
4. **Bake the Zucchini:**
   - Cover with foil and bake for 20 minutes.
   - Remove the foil, sprinkle with optional cheddar cheese, and bake for another 10 minutes until the zucchini is tender and the cheese is melted.
5. **Serve:**
   - Garnish with fresh cilantro and optional diced avocado and salsa.
   - Serve immediately.

13. Butternut Squash and Sage Risotto

Yield: 4 servings   Prepration time: 15 Minutes   Cooking Time: 30 Minutes

Nutritional Information (Per Serving):
- **Calories:** 250
- **Protein:** 6g
- **Carbohydrates:** 40g
- **Fats:** 8g
- **Fiber:** 4g
- **Cholesterol:** 0mg
- **Sodium:** 350mg
- **Potassium:** 600mg

Ingredients:

- **Butternut Squash:** 1 medium, peeled and diced
- **Olive Oil:** 2 tbsp
- **Onion:** 1, chopped
- **Garlic:** 3 cloves, minced
- **Arborio Rice:** 1 cup
- **Vegetable Broth:** 4 cups, low-sodium
- **White Wine:** 1/2 cup (optional)
- **Fresh Sage:** 2 tbsp, chopped
- **Salt:** 1/2 tsp
- **Black Pepper:** 1/4 tsp
- **Parmesan Cheese:** 1/4 cup, grated (optional)

Customizable Ingredients or Garnishes:
- **Fresh Thyme:** 1 tbsp, chopped (for garnish)
- **Red Pepper Flakes:** 1/4 tsp (for a spicy kick)

Instructions:

1. **Prepare the Butternut Squash:**
   - In a large pot, bring water to a boil.
   - Add diced butternut squash and cook for 10 minutes until tender.
   - Drain and set aside.
2. **Cook the Risotto:**
   - In a large skillet, heat olive oil over medium heat.
   - Add chopped onion and minced garlic, and cook for 5 minutes until softened.
   - Add Arborio rice and cook for 2 minutes, stirring constantly.
   - Add white wine (if using) and cook until absorbed.
   - Gradually add vegetable broth, one cup at a time, stirring frequently until each addition is absorbed before adding the next.
3. **Add the Butternut Squash and Sage:**
   - Stir in the cooked butternut squash, fresh sage, salt, and black pepper.
   - Cook for an additional 5 minutes until the risotto is creamy and the squash is heated through.
4. **Serve:**
   - Garnish with optional Parmesan cheese, fresh thyme, and red pepper flakes.
   - Serve immediately.

14. Mushroom and Spinach Lasagna

Yield: 6 servings Prepration time: 20 Minutes Cooking Time: 45 Minutes

Ingredients:

- **Olive Oil:** 2 tbsp
- **Onion:** 1, chopped
- **Garlic:** 3 cloves, minced
- **Mushrooms:** 2 cups, sliced
- **Fresh Spinach:** 4 cups, chopped
- **Tomato Sauce:** 3 cups, low-sodium
- **Ricotta Cheese:** 1 cup, low-fat
- **Mozzarella Cheese:** 1 cup, shredded, low-fat
- **Parmesan Cheese:** 1/4 cup, grated
- **Lasagna Noodles:** 12, whole wheat, cooked
- **Dried Oregano:** 1 tsp
- **Dried Basil:** 1 tsp
- **Salt:** 1/2 tsp
- **Black Pepper:** 1/4 tsp

Nutritional Information (Per Serving):
- Calories: 300
- Protein: 15g
- Carbohydrates: 35g
- Fats: 12g
- Fiber: 6g
- Cholesterol: 20mg
- Sodium: 450mg
- Potassium: 700mg

Customizable Ingredients or Garnishes:
- **Red Pepper Flakes:** 1/4 tsp (for a spicy kick)
- **Fresh Basil:** 2 tbsp, chopped (for garnish)

Instructions:

1. **Preheat the Oven:**
   - Preheat the oven to 375°F (190°C).
2. **Cook the Vegetables:**
   - In a large skillet, heat olive oil over medium heat.
   - Add chopped onion and minced garlic, and cook for 5 minutes until softened.
   - Add sliced mushrooms and cook for another 5 minutes until tender.
   - Stir in chopped spinach, dried oregano, dried basil, salt, and black pepper. Cook until the spinach is wilted.
3. **Assemble the Lasagna:**
   - In a baking dish, spread a thin layer of tomato sauce.
   - Layer 3 cooked lasagna noodles over the sauce.
   - Spread a layer of the mushroom and spinach mixture over the noodles.
   - Dollop with ricotta cheese and sprinkle with shredded mozzarella cheese.
   - Repeat layers, ending with a layer of tomato sauce and a sprinkle of Parmesan cheese.
4. **Bake the Lasagna:**
   - Cover with foil and bake for 30 minutes.
   - Remove the foil and bake for an additional 15 minutes until the cheese is melted and bubbly.
5. **Serve:**
   - Garnish with optional red pepper flakes and fresh basil.
   - Serve immediately.

15. Greek-Style Stuffed Tomatoes

Yield: 4 servings | Prepration time: 15 Minutes | Cooking Time: 30 Minutes

Ingredients:

- **Large Tomatoes:** 4, tops cut off and insides scooped out
- **Quinoa:** 1 cup, cooked
- **Olive Oil:** 2 tbsp
- **Onion:** 1, chopped
- **Garlic:** 2 cloves, minced
- **Spinach:** 2 cups, chopped
- **Feta Cheese:** 1/4 cup, crumbled, low-fat
- **Kalamata Olives:** 1/4 cup, chopped
- **Dried Oregano:** 1 tsp
- **Dried Basil:** 1 tsp
- **Salt:** 1/2 tsp
- **Black Pepper:** 1/4 tsp

Nutritional Information (Per Serving):
- **Calories:** 180
- **Protein:** 6g
- **Carbohydrates:** 20g
- **Fats:** 8g
- **Fiber:** 4g
- **Cholesterol:** 10mg
- **Sodium:** 350mg
- **Potassium:** 600mg

Customizable Ingredients or Garnishes:
- **Red Pepper Flakes:** 1/4 tsp (for a spicy kick)
- **Fresh Parsley:** 2 tbsp, chopped (for garnish)

Instructions:

1. **Preheat the Oven:**
   - Preheat the oven to 375°F (190°C).
2. **Prepare the Filling:**
   - In a large skillet, heat olive oil over medium heat.
   - Add chopped onion and minced garlic, and cook for 5 minutes until softened.
   - Add chopped spinach, cooked quinoa, dried oregano, dried basil, salt, and black pepper. Cook until the spinach is wilted.
   - Stir in crumbled feta cheese and chopped Kalamata olives.
3. **Stuff the Tomatoes:**
   - Spoon the filling into the hollowed-out tomatoes.
   - Place the stuffed tomatoes in a baking dish.
4. **Bake the Tomatoes:**
   - Bake for 25-30 minutes until the tomatoes are tender and the filling is heated through.
5. **Serve:**
   - Garnish with optional red pepper flakes and fresh parsley.
   - Serve immediately.

16. Lentil Shepherd's Pie

Yield: 6 servings   Prepration time: 20 Minutes   Cooking Time: 45 Minutes

Ingredients:

- **Olive Oil:** 2 tbsp
- **Onion:** 1, chopped
- **Garlic:** 3 cloves, minced
- **Carrots:** 2, diced
- **Celery:** 2 stalks, diced
- **Lentils:** 1 cup, dried
- **Vegetable Broth:** 4 cups, low-sodium
- **Tomato Paste:** 2 tbsp
- **Dried Thyme:** 1 tsp
- **Dried Rosemary:** 1 tsp
- **Peas:** 1 cup, frozen
- **Corn:** 1 cup, frozen
- **Potatoes:** 4 large, peeled and cubed
- **Unsweetened Almond Milk:** 1/2 cup
- **Salt:** 1/2 tsp
- **Black Pepper:** 1/4 tsp

Nutritional Information (Per Serving):
- Calories: 280
- Protein: 10g
- Carbohydrates: 50g
- Fats: 6g
- Fiber: 10g
- Cholesterol: 0mg
- Sodium: 400mg
- Potassium: 900mg

Customizable Ingredients or Garnishes:
- **Nutritional Yeast:** 2 tbsp (for a cheesy flavor)
- **Chopped Fresh Parsley:** 2 tbsp (for garnish)
- **Red Pepper Flakes:** 1/4 tsp (for a spicy kick)

Instructions:

1. **Prepare the Potatoes:**
   - In a large pot, bring water to a boil.
   - Add cubed potatoes and cook for 15-20 minutes until tender.
   - Drain and mash with almond milk, salt, and black pepper. Set aside.
2. **Cook the Vegetables and Lentils:**
   - In a large skillet, heat olive oil over medium heat.
   - Add chopped onion, minced garlic, diced carrots, and diced celery. Cook for 5 minutes until softened.
   - Add lentils, vegetable broth, tomato paste, dried thyme, and dried rosemary. Bring to a boil, then reduce heat and simmer for 20 minutes until lentils are tender.
   - Stir in frozen peas and corn, and cook for an additional 5 minutes.
3. **Assemble the Shepherd's Pie:**
   - Preheat the oven to 375°F (190°C).
   - Transter the lentil mixture to a baking dish.
   - Spread the mashed potatoes evenly over the top.
4. **Bake the Shepherd's Pie:**
   - Bake for 20-25 minutes until the top is golden and the filling is bubbling.
5. **Serve:**
   - Garnish with optional nutritional yeast, chopped fresh parsley, and red pepper flakes.
   - Serve immediately.

17. Grilled Vegetable and Hummus Wraps

Yield: 4 servings   Prepration time: 15 Minutes   Cooking Time: 10 Minutes

Ingredients:

- **Whole Wheat Tortillas:** 4
- **Red Bell Pepper:** 1, sliced
- **Zucchini:** 1, sliced
- **Eggplant:** 1 small, sliced
- **Olive Oil:** 2 tbsp
- **Hummus:** 1 cup, low-fat
- **Spinach:** 2 cups, fresh
- **Salt:** 1/2 tsp
- **Black Pepper:** 1/4 tsp

Customizable Ingredients or Garnishes:
- **Avocado:** 1, sliced
- **Feta Cheese:** 1/4 cup, crumbled (optional)
- **Red Pepper Flakes:** 1/4 tsp (for a spicy kick)

Nutritional Information (Per Serving):
- Calories: 250
- Protein: 7g
- Carbohydrates: 30g
- Fats: 12g
- Fiber: 8g
- Cholesterol: 0mg
- Sodium: 400mg
- Potassium: 600mg

Instructions:

1. **Preheat the Grill:**
   - Preheat the grill to medium-high heat.
2. **Grill the Vegetables:**
   - In a large bowl, toss sliced red bell pepper, zucchini, and eggplant with olive oil, salt, and black pepper.
   - Grill the vegetables for 4-5 minutes on each side until tender and slightly charred.
3. **Assemble the Wraps:**
   - Spread a generous layer of hummus on each tortilla.
   - Layer with grilled vegetables and fresh spinach.
4. **Serve:**
   - Roll up the wraps tightly.
   - Garnish with optional avocado slices, feta cheese, and red pepper flakes.
   - Serve immediately.

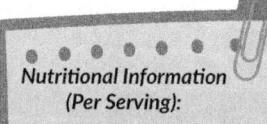

18. Black Bean and Corn Stuffed Sweet Potatoes

Yield: 4 servings **Prepration time:** 10 Minutes **Cooking Time:** 45 Minutes

Ingredients:

- **Sweet Potatoes:** 4 medium
- **Olive Oil:** 1 tbsp
- **Black Beans:** 1 can (15 oz), drained and rinsed
- **Corn Kernels:** 1 cup, cooked
- **Red Onion:** 1/4 cup, finely chopped
- **Cumin:** 1 tsp
- **Chili Powder:** 1 tsp
- **Salt:** 1/2 tsp
- **Black Pepper:** 1/4 tsp
- **Fresh Cilantro:** 1/4 cup, chopped
- **Lime Juice:** 1 tbsp

Nutritional Information (Per Serving):
- Calories: 300
- Protein: 7g
- Carbohydrates: 55g
- Fats: 7g
- Fiber: 12g
- Cholesterol: 0mg
- Sodium: 400mg
- Potassium: 800mg

Customizable Ingredients or Garnishes:
- **Avocado:** 1, diced
- **Greek Yogurt:** 1/4 cup, low-fat (for a creamy topping)
- **Salsa:** 1/2 cup (for serving)

Instructions:

1. **Preheat the Oven:**
   - Preheat the oven to 400°F (200°C).
2. **Bake the Sweet Potatoes:**
   - Wash and pierce the sweet potatoes with a fork.
   - Place on a baking sheet and bake for 45 minutes until tender.
3. **Prepare the Filling:**
   - In a large skillet, heat olive oil over medium heat.
   - Add finely chopped red onion and cook for 5 minutes until softened.
   - Add black beans, corn, cumin, chili powder, salt, and black pepper. Cook for another 5 minutes.
   - Stir in fresh cilantro and lime juice.
4. **Stuff the Sweet Potatoes:**
   - Slice the baked sweet potatoes open and fluff the insides with a fork.
   - Spoon the black bean and corn mixture into the sweet potatoes.
5. **Serve:**
   - Garnish with optional diced avocado, Greek yogurt, and salsa.
   - Serve immediately.

19. Veggie-Packed Buddha Bowl

Yield: 4 servings Prepration time: 15 Minutes Cooking Time: 20 Minutes

Ingredients:

- **Quinoa:** 1 cup, uncooked
- **Water:** 2 cups
- **Olive Oil:** 2 tbsp
- **Broccoli Florets:** 2 cups
- **Carrot:** 2, sliced
- **Red Bell Pepper:** 1, sliced
- **Chickpeas:** 1 can (15 oz), drained and rinsed
- **Spinach:** 2 cups, fresh
- **Avocado:** 1, sliced
- **Tahini:** 1/4 cup
- **Lemon Juice:** 2 tbsp
- **Garlic:** 1 clove, minced
- **Water:** 2-3 tbsp (for thinning)
- **Salt:** 1/2 tsp
- **Black Pepper:** 1/4 tsp

Nutritional Information (Per Serving):
- **Calories:** 350
- **Protein:** 12g
- **Carbohydrates:** 45g
- **Fats:** 15g
- **Fiber:** 10g
- **Cholesterol:** 0mg
- **Sodium:** 300mg
- **Potassium:** 800mg

Customizable Ingredients or Garnishes:
- **Hummus:** 1/2 cup (for added flavor)
- **Red Pepper Flakes:** 1/4 tsp (for a spicy kick)
- **Pumpkin Seeds:** 2 tbsp (for added crunch)

Instructions:

1. **Cook the Quinoa:**
   - Rinse the quinoa under cold water.
   - In a medium pot, bring water to a boil.
   - Add quinoa, reduce heat to low, cover, and simmer for 15 minutes, or until the water is absorbed.
   - Fluff with a fork and set aside.
2. **Roast the Vegetables:**
   - Preheat the oven to 400°F (200°C).
   - In a large bowl, toss broccoli florets, sliced carrots, and sliced red bell pepper with olive oil, salt, and black pepper.
   - Spread the vegetables on a baking sheet and roast for 20 minutes until tender.
3. **Prepare the Tahini Dressing:**
   - In a small bowl, whisk together tahini, lemon juice, minced garlic, and water until smooth.
4. **Assemble the Buddha Bowl:**
   - Divide the cooked quinoa among four bowls.
   - Top with roasted vegetables, chickpeas, fresh spinach, and avocado slices.
   - Drizzle with tahini dressing.
5. **Serve:**
   - Garnish with optional hummus, red pepper flakes, and pumpkin seeds.
   - Serve immediately.

20. Spinach and Feta Stuffed Portobello Mushrooms

Yield: 4 servings Prepration time: 10 Minutes Cooking Time: 25 Minutes

Nutritional Information (Per Serving):
- **Calories:** 200
- **Protein:** 7g
- **Carbohydrates:** 15g
- **Fats:** 12g
- **Fiber:** 4g
- **Cholesterol:** 20mg
- **Sodium:** 400mg
- **Potassium:** 600mg

Ingredients:

- **Portobello Mushrooms:** 4 large, stems removed
- **Olive Oil:** 2 tbsp
- **Onion:** 1, chopped
- **Garlic:** 3 cloves, minced
- **Fresh Spinach:** 4 cups, chopped
- **Feta Cheese:** 1/2 cup, crumbled, low-fat
- **Dried Oregano:** 1 tsp
- **Salt:** 1/2 tsp
- **Black Pepper:** 1/4 tsp
- **Breadcrumbs:** 1/4 cup, whole wheat

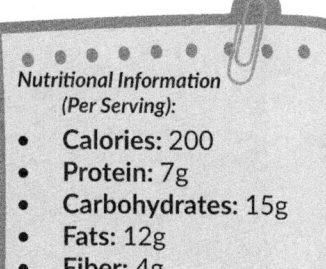

Customizable Ingredients or Garnishes:
- **Red Pepper Flakes:** 1/4 tsp (for a spicy kick)
- **Fresh Parsley:** 2 tbsp, chopped (for garnish)

Instructions:

1. **Preheat the Oven:**
   - Preheat the oven to 375°F (190°C).
2. **Prepare the Filling:**
   - In a large skillet, heat olive oil over medium heat.
   - Add chopped onion and minced garlic, and cook for 5 minutes until softened.
   - Add chopped spinach, dried oregano, salt, and black pepper. Cook until the spinach is wilted.
   - Stir in crumbled feta cheese.
3. **Stuff the Mushrooms:**
   - Spoon the spinach and feta mixture into the portobello mushrooms.
   - Sprinkle with breadcrumbs.
4. **Bake the Mushrooms:**
   - Place the stuffed mushrooms on a baking sheet.
   - Bake for 20-25 minutes until the mushrooms are tender and the filling is heated through.
5. **Serve:**
   - Garnish with optional red pepper flakes and fresh parsley.
   - Serve immediately.

CHAPTER 9. DESSERTS

1. Avocado Chocolate Mousse

🛎 Yield: 4 servings ⏱ Prepration time: 10 Minutes 👨‍🍳 Cooking Time: 0 Minutes

Nutritional Information (Per Serving):
- Calories: 210
- Protein: 3g
- Carbohydrates: 22g
- Fats: 14g
- Fiber: 7g
- Cholesterol: 0mg
- Sodium: 60mg
- Potassium: 540mg

Ingredients:

- **Ripe Avocados:** 2, pitted and peeled
- **Cocoa Powder:** 1/4 cup, unsweetened
- **Maple Syrup:** 1/4 cup
- **Vanilla Extract:** 1 tsp
- **Almond Milk:** 1/4 cup, unsweetened
- **Salt:** 1/8 tsp

Customizable Ingredients or Garnishes:
- **Fresh Berries:** 1/2 cup (for garnish)
- **Mint Leaves:** For garnish
- **Chopped Nuts:** 2 tbsp (for garnish)

Instructions:

1. **Blend Ingredients:**
   - In a blender or food processor, combine avocados, cocoa powder, maple syrup, vanilla extract, almond milk, and salt.
   - Blend until smooth and creamy.
2. **Chill and Serve:**
   - Spoon the mousse into serving bowls.
   - Chill in the refrigerator for at least 30 minutes before serving.
   - Garnish with fresh berries, mint leaves, and chopped nuts, if desired.

2. Berry Chia Seed Pudding

Yield: 4 servings Prepration time: 10 Minutes Cooking Time: 0 Minutes (refrigeration time: 4 hours or overnight)

Ingredients:

- **Chia Seeds:** 1/2 cup
- **Almond Milk:** 2 cups, unsweetened
- **Maple Syrup:** 2 tbsp
- **Vanilla Extract:** 1 tsp
- **Mixed Berries:** 1 cup, fresh or frozen

Customizable Ingredients or Garnishes:
- **Coconut Flakes:** 2 tbsp (for garnish)
- **Nuts or Seeds:** 2 tbsp (for garnish)
- **Mint Leaves:** For garnish

Nutritional Information (Per Serving):
- **Calories:** 150
- **Protein:** 4g
- **Carbohydrates:** 20g
- **Fats:** 7g
- **Fiber:** 8g
- **Cholesterol:** 0mg
- **Sodium:** 50mg
- **Potassium:** 200mg

Instructions:

1. **Mix Ingredients:**
   - In a bowl, combine chia seeds, almond milk, maple syrup, and vanilla extract.
   - Stir well to combine.
2. **Refrigerate:**
   - Cover the bowl and refrigerate for at least 4 hours or overnight, stirring occasionally to prevent clumping.
3. **Serve:**
   - Stir the pudding before serving.
   - Divide into serving bowls and top with mixed berries and optional garnishes.

3. Almond Flour Blueberry Muffins

Yield: 12 muffins Prepration time: 15 Minutes Cooking Time: 25 Minutes

Ingredients:

- **Almond Flour:** 2 cups
- **Baking Soda:** 1 tsp
- **Salt:** 1/4 tsp
- **Eggs:** 3 large
- **Maple Syrup:** 1/4 cup
- **Vanilla Extract:** 1 tsp
- **Apple Cider Vinegar:** 1 tbsp
- **Blueberries:** 1 cup, fresh or frozen

Customizable Ingredients or Garnishes:
- **Lemon Zest:** 1 tsp (for added flavor)
- **Chopped Nuts:** 1/4 cup (for added texture)
- **Cinnamon:** 1 tsp (for added spice)

Nutritional Information (Per Serving):
- **Calories:** 180
- **Protein:** 6g
- **Carbohydrates:** 12g
- **Fats:** 12g
- **Fiber:** 3g
- **Cholesterol:** 40mg
- **Sodium:** 150mg
- **Potassium:** 100mg

Instructions:

1. **Preheat the Oven:**
   - Preheat the oven to 350°F (175°C).
   - Line a muffin tin with paper liners or lightly grease with olive oil.
2. **Mix Dry Ingredients:**
   - In a large bowl, combine almond flour, baking soda, and salt.
3. **Mix Wet Ingredients:**
   - In a separate bowl, whisk together eggs, maple syrup, vanilla extract, and apple cider vinegar.
4. **Combine and Add Blueberries:**
   - Add the wet ingredients to the dry ingredients and mix until just combined.
   - Fold in the blueberries.
5. **Bake the Muffins:**
   - Divide the batter evenly among the muffin cups.
   - Bake for 20-25 minutes until a toothpick inserted into the center comes out clean.
6. **Serve:**
   - Let the muffins cool in the pan for 10 minutes, then transfer to a wire rack to cool completely.
   - Serve warm or at room temperature.

4. Coconut Milk Panna Cotta

Yield: 4 servings *Prepration time: 10 Minutes* *Cooking Time: 10 Minutes (refrigeration time: 4 hours or overnight)*

Ingredients:

- **Coconut Milk:** 2 cups, full-fat
- **Maple Syrup:** 1/4 cup
- **Vanilla Extract:** 1 tsp
- **Agar Agar Powder:** 1 tsp (or 1 tbsp gelatin powder)
- **Mixed Berries:** 1 cup (for serving)

Customizable Ingredients or Garnishes:
- **Coconut Flakes:** 2 tbsp (for garnish)
- **Mint Leaves:** For garnish
- **Chopped Nuts:** 2 tbsp (for garnish)

Nutritional Information (Per Serving):
- Calories: 220
- Protein: 2g
- Carbohydrates: 20g
- Fats: 15g
- Fiber: 2g
- Cholesterol: 0mg
- Sodium: 20mg
- Potassium: 150mg

Instructions:

1. **Heat Coconut Milk:**
   - In a saucepan, combine coconut milk, maple syrup, and vanilla extract.
   - Bring to a simmer over medium heat.
2. **Add Agar Agar:**
   - Sprinkle agar agar powder over the coconut milk mixture and whisk continuously until fully dissolved, about 3-5 minutes.
3. **Pour and Chill:**
   - Pour the mixture into ramekins or serving glasses.
   - Refrigerate for at least 4 hours or overnight until set.
4. **Serve:**
   - Top with mixed berries and optional coconut flakes, mint leaves, and chopped nuts.
   - Serve chilled.

5. Oatmeal Raisin Cookies

🔔 Yield: 24 cookies ⚙ Prepration time: 15 Minutes 🍳 Cooking Time: 10 Minutes

Nutritional Information (Per Serving):
- **Calories:** 100
- **Protein:** 2g
- **Carbohydrates:** 15g
- **Fats:** 4g
- **Fiber:** 2g
- **Cholesterol:** 0mg
- **Sodium:** 80mg
- **Potassium:** 100mg

Ingredients:

- **Rolled Oats:** 2 cups
- **Whole Wheat Flour:** 1 cup
- **Baking Soda:** 1 tsp
- **Cinnamon:** 1 tsp
- **Salt:** 1/2 tsp
- **Coconut Oil:** 1/2 cup, melted
- **Maple Syrup:** 1/2 cup
- **Vanilla Extract:** 1 tsp
- **Raisins:** 1 cup

Customizable Ingredients or Garnishes:
- **Chopped Nuts:** 1/2 cup (for added texture)
- **Dark Chocolate Chips:** 1/2 cup (for added flavor)
- **Shredded Coconut:** 1/4 cup (for added texture)

Instructions:

1. **Preheat the Oven:**
   - Preheat the oven to 350°F (175°C).
   - Line a baking sheet with parchment paper.
2. **Mix Dry Ingredients:**
   - In a large bowl, combine rolled oats, whole wheat flour, baking soda, cinnamon, and salt.
3. **Mix Wet Ingredients:**
   - In a separate bowl, whisk together melted coconut oil, maple syrup, and vanilla extract.
4. **Combine and Add Raisins:**
   - Add the wet ingredients to the dry ingredients and mix until just combined.
   - Fold in the raisins.
5. **Scoop and Bake:**
   - Scoop tablespoon-sized portions of dough onto the prepared baking sheet.
   - Bake for 8-10 minutes until the edges are golden.
6. **Cool and Serve:**
   - Let the cookies cool on the baking sheet for 5 minutes, then transfer to a wire rack to cool completely.
   - Serve and enjoy.

6. Lemon Yogurt Parfaits

Yield: 4 servings Prepration time: 10 Minutes Cooking Time: 0 Minutes

Nutritional Information (Per Serving):
- **Calories:** 180
- **Protein:** 10g
- **Carbohydrates:** 25g
- **Fats:** 5g
- **Fiber:** 3g
- **Cholesterol:** 5mg
- **Sodium:** 60mg
- **Potassium:** 200mg

Ingredients:

- **Greek Yogurt:** 2 cups, low-fat
- **Lemon Juice:** 2 tbsp
- **Lemon Zest:** 1 tbsp
- **Maple Syrup:** 2 tbsp
- **Granola:** 1 cup, low-sugar
- **Fresh Berries:** 1 cup

Customizable Ingredients or Garnishes:
- **Chopped Nuts:** 1/4 cup (for added texture)
- **Mint Leaves:** For garnish
- **Shredded Coconut:** 2 tbsp (for added texture)

Instructions:

1. **Mix Yogurt:**
   - In a bowl, combine Greek yogurt, lemon juice, lemon zest, and maple syrup. Mix until smooth.
2. **Assemble the Parfaits:**
   - In serving glasses, layer the lemon yogurt, granola, and fresh berries.
3. **Serve:**
   - Garnish with optional chopped nuts, mint leaves, and shredded coconut.
   - Serve immediately.

7. Carrot Cake Energy Bites

Yield: 12 bites   Prepration time: 15 Minutes   Cooking Time: 0 Minutes

Nutritional Information (Per Serving):
- **Calories:** 100
- **Protein:** 3g
- **Carbohydrates:** 12g
- **Fats:** 5g
- **Fiber:** 2g
- **Cholesterol:** 0mg
- **Sodium:** 20mg
- **Potassium:** 100mg

Ingredients:

- **Rolled Oats:** 1 cup
- **Carrot:** 1 large, grated
- **Almond Butter:** 1/2 cup
- **Maple Syrup:** 1/4 cup
- **Cinnamon:** 1 tsp
- **Nutmeg:** 1/4 tsp
- **Vanilla Extract:** 1 tsp
- **Chia Seeds:** 2 tbsp
- **Raisins:** 1/4 cup

Customizable Ingredients or Garnishes:
- **Shredded Coconut:** 1/4 cup (for added texture)
- **Chopped Nuts:** 1/4 cup (for added texture)
- **Ground Flaxseed:** 2 tbsp (for added nutrition)

Instructions:

1. **Mix Ingredients:**
   - In a large bowl, combine rolled oats, grated carrot, almond butter, maple syrup, cinnamon, nutmeg, vanilla extract, chia seeds, and raisins. Mix until well combined.
2. **Form Bites:**
   - Roll the mixture into tablespoon-sized balls.
3. **Chill and Serve:**
   - Place the energy bites on a baking sheet and refrigerate for at least 30 minutes to firm up.
   - Serve chilled.

8. Mango Sorbet

Yield: 4 servings **Prepration time:** 10 Minutes **Cooking Time:** 0 Minutes (freezing time: 4 hours)

Ingredients:

- **Mangoes:** 4 cups, peeled and chopped (about 2 large mangoes)
- **Lime Juice:** 2 tbsp
- **Maple Syrup:** 2 tbsp
- **Water:** 1/2 cup

Nutritional Information (Per Serving):
- **Calories:** 90
- **Protein:** 1g
- **Carbohydrates:** 24g
- **Fats:** 0.5g
- **Fiber:** 2g
- **Cholesterol:** 0mg
- **Sodium:** 5mg
- **Potassium:** 180mg

Instructions:

1. **Blend Ingredients:**
   - In a blender, combine mangoes, lime juice, maple syrup, and water.
   - Blend until smooth.
2. **Freeze:**
   - Pour the mixture into a shallow dish and freeze for about 4 hours, stirring every hour to break up ice crystals.
   - Alternatively, use an ice cream maker according to the manufacturer's instructions.
3. **Serve:**
   - Scoop the sorbet into bowls and serve immediately.

9. Apple Cinnamon Quinoa Bake

Yield: 6 servings   *Prepration time:* 15 Minutes   *Cooking Time:* 45 Minutes

Ingredients:

- **Quinoa:** 1 cup, uncooked
- **Almond Milk:** 2 cups, unsweetened
- **Apples:** 2, peeled, cored, and diced
- **Maple Syrup:** 1/4 cup
- **Cinnamon:** 1 tsp
- **Vanilla Extract:** 1 tsp
- **Chopped Nuts:** 1/4 cup (optional)

Nutritional Information (Per Serving):
- **Calories:** 180
- **Protein:** 5g
- **Carbohydrates:** 34g
- **Fats:** 3g
- **Fiber:** 4g
- **Cholesterol:** 40mg
- **Sodium:** 30mg
- **Potassium:** 200mg

Instructions:

1. **Preheat the Oven:**
   - Preheat the oven to 350°F (175°C).
2. **Mix Ingredients:**
   - In a large bowl, combine quinoa, almond milk, diced apples, maple syrup, cinnamon, and vanilla extract.
   - Mix well and pour into a greased baking dish.
3. **Bake:**
   - Bake for 45 minutes until the quinoa is cooked and the top is golden brown.
4. **Serve:**
   - Serve warm, optionally topped with chopped nuts.

10. Chia Seed and Coconut Pudding

Yield: 4 servings Prepration time: 10 Minutes Cooking Time: 0 Minutes (refrigeration time: 4 hours or overnight)

Ingredients:

- **Chia Seeds:** 1/2 cup
- **Coconut Milk:** 2 cups, unsweetened
- **Maple Syrup:** 2 tbsp
- **Vanilla Extract:** 1 tsp

Customizable Ingredients or Garnishes:
- **Fresh Berries:** 1/2 cup (for garnish)
- **Shredded Coconut:** 2 tbsp (for garnish)
- **Mint Leaves:** For garnish

Nutritional Information (Per Serving):
- **Calories:** 180
- **Protein:** 4g
- **Carbohydrates:** 15g
- **Fats:** 12g
- **Fiber:** 6g
- **Cholesterol:** 0mg
- **Sodium:** 20mg
- **Potassium:** 200mg

Instructions:

1. **Mix Ingredients:**
   - In a bowl, combine chia seeds, coconut milk, maple syrup, and vanilla extract.
   - Stir well to combine.
2. **Refrigerate:**
   - Cover the bowl and refrigerate for at least 4 hours or overnight, stirring occasionally to prevent clumping.
3. **Serve:**
   - Stir the pudding before serving.
   - Divide into serving bowls and top with fresh berries and optional garnishes.

11. Vegan Banana Bread

Yield: 10 slices   Prepration time: 15 Minutes   Cooking Time: 50 Minutes

Nutritional Information (Per Serving):
- **Calories:** 180
- **Protein:** 3g
- **Carbohydrates:** 28g
- **Fats:** 7g
- **Fiber:** 3g
- **Cholesterol:** 0mg
- **Sodium:** 150mg
- **Potassium:** 200mg

Ingredients:

- **Ripe Bananas:** 3 large, mashed
- **Maple Syrup:** 1/4 cup
- **Coconut Oil:** 1/4 cup, melted
- **Vanilla Extract:** 1 tsp
- **Whole Wheat Flour:** 1 1/2 cups
- **Baking Soda:** 1 tsp
- **Cinnamon:** 1 tsp
- **Salt:** 1/4 tsp
- **Chopped Nuts or Chocolate Chips:** 1/2 cup (optional)

Instructions:

1. **Preheat the Oven:**
   - Preheat the oven to 350°F (175°C).
   - Grease a loaf pan or line it with parchment paper.
2. **Mix Wet Ingredients:**
   - In a large bowl, combine mashed bananas, maple syrup, melted coconut oil, and vanilla extract. Mix well.
3. **Mix Dry Ingredients:**
   - In a separate bowl, combine whole wheat flour, baking soda, cinnamon, and salt.
4. **Combine:**
   - Add the dry ingredients to the wet ingredients and mix until just combined.
   - Fold in chopped nuts or chocolate chips if using.
5. **Bake:**
   - Pour the batter into the prepared loaf pan.
   - Bake for 50-60 minutes until a toothpick inserted into the center comes out clean.
6. **Cool and Serve:**
   - Let the banana bread cool in the pan for 10 minutes, then transfer to a wire rack to cool completely.
   - Slice and serve.

12. Raspberry and Almond Crumble

Yield: 6 servings   Prepration time: 15 Minutes   Cooking Time: 30 Minutes

Nutritional Information (Per Serving):
- **Calories:** 220
- **Protein:** 4g
- **Carbohydrates:** 25g
- **Fats:** 12g
- **Fiber:** 6g
- **Cholesterol:** 0mg
- **Sodium:** 70mg
- **Potassium:** 200mg

Ingredients:

- **Raspberries:** 4 cups, fresh or frozen
- **Maple Syrup:** 1/4 cup
- **Lemon Juice:** 2 tbsp
- **Almond Flour:** 1 cup
- **Rolled Oats:** 1/2 cup
- **Coconut Oil:** 1/4 cup, melted
- **Cinnamon:** 1 tsp
- **Salt:** 1/4 tsp
- **Sliced Almonds:** 1/4 cup

Instructions:

1. **Preheat the Oven:**
   - Preheat the oven to 350°F (175°C).
2. **Prepare the Filling:**
   - In a bowl, combine raspberries, maple syrup, and lemon juice. Mix well.
   - Pour the raspberry mixture into a baking dish.
3. **Prepare the Crumble Topping:**
   - In a separate bowl, combine almond flour, rolled oats, melted coconut oil, cinnamon, and salt.
   - Mix until the mixture resembles coarse crumbs.
   - Stir in sliced almonds.
4. **Assemble and Bake:**
   - Sprinkle the crumble topping evenly over the raspberries.
   - Bake for 25-30 minutes until the topping is golden brown and the raspberries are bubbly.
5. **Serve:**
   - Let the crumble cool for 10 minutes before serving.
   - Serve warm.

13. Pineapple and Coconut Ice Pops

Yield: 6 servings | Prepration time: 10 Minutes | Cooking Time: 0 Minutes (freezing time: 4 hours)

Ingredients:

- **Pineapple:** 2 cups, chopped (fresh or canned, drained)
- **Coconut Milk:** 1 cup, unsweetened
- **Maple Syrup:** 2 tbsp
- **Lime Juice:** 1 tbsp

Instructions:

1. **Blend Ingredients:**
   - In a blender, combine pineapple, coconut milk, maple syrup, and lime juice.
   - Blend until smooth.
2. **Pour and Freeze:**
   - Pour the mixture into ice pop molds.
   - Freeze for at least 4 hours until solid.
3. **Serve:**
   - Remove from molds and serve immediately.

Nutritional Information (Per Serving):
- **Calories:** 70
- **Protein:** 1g
- **Carbohydrates:** 12g
- **Fats:** 3g
- **Fiber:** 1g
- **Cholesterol:** 0mg
- **Sodium:** 10mg
- **Potassium:** 100mg

14. Chocolate Avocado Brownies

Yield: 12 brownies Prepration time: 15 Minutes Cooking Time: 25 Minutes

Ingredients:

- **Ripe Avocados:** 2, pitted and peeled
- **Maple Syrup:** 1/2 cup
- **Vanilla Extract:** 1 tsp
- **Cocoa Powder:** 1/2 cup, unsweetened
- **Whole Wheat Flour:** 1/2 cup
- **Baking Powder:** 1 tsp
- **Salt:** 1/4 tsp
- **Dark Chocolate Chips:** 1/4 cup (optional)

Nutritional Information (Per Serving):
- **Calories:** 140
- **Protein:** 2g
- **Carbohydrates:** 20g
- **Fats:** 7g
- **Fiber:** 3g
- **Cholesterol:** 0mg
- **Sodium:** 100mg
- **Potassium:** 200mg

Instructions:

1. **Preheat the Oven:**
   - Preheat the oven to 350°F (175°C).
   - Line a baking dish with parchment paper.
2. **Blend Wet Ingredients:**
   - In a blender or food processor, combine avocados, maple syrup, and vanilla extract. Blend until smooth.
3. **Mix Dry Ingredients:**
   - In a bowl, combine cocoa powder, whole wheat flour, baking powder, and salt.
4. **Combine:**
   - Add the wet ingredients to the dry ingredients and mix until just combined.
   - Fold in dark chocolate chips if using.
5. **Bake:**
   - Pour the batter into the prepared baking dish.
   - Bake for 20-25 minutes until a toothpick inserted into the center comes out clean.
6. **Cool and Serve:**
   - Let the brownies cool in the dish for 10 minutes, then transfer to a wire rack to cool completely.
   - Cut into squares and serve.

15. Blueberry and Lemon Zest Greek Yogurt Bars

Yield: 8 bars   *Prepration time: 15 Minutes*   *Cooking Time: 0 Minutes (freezing time: 2 hours)*

Ingredients:

- **Greek Yogurt:** 2 cups, low-fat
- **Maple Syrup:** 1/4 cup
- **Lemon Zest:** 1 tbsp
- **Blueberries:** 1 cup, fresh or frozen

Nutritional Information (Per Serving):
- **Calories:** 80
- **Protein:** 6g
- **Carbohydrates:** 12g
- **Fats:** 1g
- **Fiber:** 1g
- **Cholesterol:** 5mg
- **Sodium:** 30mg
- **Potassium:** 100mg

Instructions:

1. **Mix Ingredients:**
   - In a bowl, combine Greek yogurt, maple syrup, and lemon zest. Mix well.
2. **Prepare the Bars:**
   - Line a baking dish with parchment paper.
   - Spread the yogurt mixture evenly in the dish.
   - Sprinkle blueberries on top, pressing them gently into the yogurt.
3. **Freeze:**
   - Freeze for at least 2 hours until firm.
4. **Serve:**
   - Cut into bars and serve immediately.

CHAPTER 10. BEVERAGES AND SMOOTHIES

1. Green Detox Smoothie

🍽️ Yield: 2 servings   ⚙️ Prepration time: 10 Minutes   🍳 Cooking Time: 0 Minutes

Ingredients:

- **Kale:** 1 cup, chopped
- **Spinach:** 1 cup, chopped
- **Cucumber:** 1, chopped
- **Green Apple:** 1, cored and chopped
- **Lemon Juice:** 2 tbsp
- **Ginger:** 1 inch, peeled and grated
- **Water:** 1 cup
- **Ice Cubes:** 1 cup

Nutritional Information (Per Serving):
- **Calories:** 60
- **Protein:** 2g
- **Carbohydrates:** 15g
- **Fats:** 0.5g
- **Fiber:** 4g
- **Cholesterol:** 0mg
- **Sodium:** 35mg
- **Potassium:** 350mg

Instructions:

1. **Blend Ingredients:**
   - Combine kale, spinach, cucumber, green apple, lemon juice, ginger, water, and ice cubes in a blender.
   - Blend until smooth.
2. **Serve:**
   - Pour into glasses and serve immediately.

2. Berry Protein Shake

🍽️ Yield: 2 servings   ⚙️ Prepration time: 5 Minutes   🍳 Cooking Time: 0 Minutes

Ingredients:

- **Mixed Berries:** 1 cup, fresh or frozen
- **Protein Powder:** 1 scoop (plant-based or whey)
- **Almond Milk:** 1 cup, unsweetened
- **Greek Yogurt:** 1/2 cup, low-fat
- **Chia Seeds:** 1 tbsp
- **Honey:** 1 tbsp (optional)

Nutritional Information (Per Serving):
- **Calories:** 180
- **Protein:** 18g
- **Carbohydrates:** 20g
- **Fats:** 5g
- **Fiber:** 6g
- **Cholesterol:** 5mg
- **Sodium:** 100mg
- **Potassium:** 400mg

Instructions:

1. **Blend Ingredients:**
   - Combine mixed berries, protein powder, almond milk, Greek yogurt, chia seeds, and honey (if using) in a blender.
   - Blend until smooth.
2. **Serve:**
   - Pour into glasses and serve immediately.

3. Coconut Water and Pineapple Cooler

Yield: 2 servings Prepration time: 5 Minutes Cooking Time: 0 Minutes

Nutritional Information (Per Serving):
- Calories: 70
- Protein: 1g
- Carbohydrates: 17g
- Fats: 0.5g
- Fiber: 2g
- Cholesterol: 0mg
- Sodium: 60mg
- Potassium: 250mg

Ingredients:

- **Coconut Water:** 2 cups
- **Pineapple Chunks:** 1 cup, fresh or frozen
- **Lime Juice:** 2 tbsp
- **Mint Leaves:** 2 tbsp, chopped
- **Ice Cubes:** 1 cup

Instructions:

1. **Blend Ingredients:**
   - Combine coconut water, pineapple chunks, lime juice, mint leaves, and ice cubes in a blender.
   - Blend until smooth.
2. **Serve:**
   - Pour into glasses and serve immediately.

4. Spinach and Avocado Smoothie

Yield: 2 servings Prepration time: 5 Minutes Cooking Time: 0 Minutes

Nutritional Information (Per Serving):
- Calories: 150
- Protein: 3g
- Carbohydrates: 25g
- Fats: 7g
- Fiber: 7g
- Cholesterol: 0mg
- Sodium: 60mg
- Potassium: 500mg

Ingredients:

- **Spinach:** 2 cups, fresh
- **Avocado:** 1, pitted and peeled
- **Banana:** 1, sliced
- **Almond Milk:** 1 cup, unsweetened
- **Lime Juice:** 1 tbsp
- **Ice Cubes:** 1 cup

Instructions:

1. **Blend Ingredients:**
   - Combine spinach, avocado, banana, almond milk, lime juice, and ice cubes in a blender.
   - Blend until smooth.
2. **Serve:**
   - Pour into glasses and serve immediately.

5. Chia Seed Lemonade

Yield: 2 servings | Prepration time: 10 Minutes | Cooking Time: 0 Minutes

Nutritional Information (Per Serving):
- Calories: 70
- Protein: 1g
- Carbohydrates: 15g
- Fats: 3g
- Fiber: 4g
- Cholesterol: 0mg
- Sodium: 10mg
- Potassium: 50mg

Ingredients:

- **Lemon Juice:** 1/4 cup (about 2 lemons)
- **Water:** 2 cups
- **Chia Seeds:** 2 tbsp
- **Maple Syrup:** 2 tbsp
- **Ice Cubes:** 1 cup

Instructions:

1. **Prepare Chia Seeds:**
   - In a glass, combine chia seeds and 1/2 cup of water.
   - Let it sit for 10 minutes until the chia seeds absorb the water and swell.
2. **Mix Lemonade:**
   - In a pitcher, combine lemon juice, remaining water, maple syrup, and chia seed mixture.
   - Stir well.
3. **Serve:**
   - Pour into glasses over ice cubes and serve immediately.

6. Almond Butter and Banana Smoothie

Yield: 2 servings | Prepration time: 5 Minutes | Cooking Time: 0 Minutes

Nutritional Information (Per Serving):
- Calories: 220
- Protein: 7g
- Carbohydrates: 30g
- Fats: 9g
- Fiber: 4g
- Cholesterol: 5mg
- Sodium: 80mg
- Potassium: 450mg

Ingredients:

- **Banana:** 2, sliced
- **Almond Butter:** 2 tbsp
- **Almond Milk:** 1 cup, unsweetened
- **Greek Yogurt:** 1/2 cup, low-fat
- **Honey:** 1 tbsp (optional)
- **Ice Cubes:** 1 cup

Instructions:

1. **Blend Ingredients:**
   - Combine banana, almond butter, almond milk, Greek yogurt, honey (if using), and ice cubes in a blender.
   - Blend until smooth.
2. **Serve:**
   - Pour into glasses and serve immediately.

7. Blueberry and Oat Smoothie

Yield: 2 servings **Prepration time:** 5 Minutes **Cooking Time:** 0 Minutes

Nutritional Information (Per Serving):
- Calories: 170
- Protein: 7g
- Carbohydrates: 30g
- Fats: 3g
- Fiber: 5g
- Cholesterol: 5mg
- Sodium: 70mg
- Potassium: 300mg

Ingredients:

- **Blueberries:** 1 cup, fresh or frozen
- **Rolled Oats:** 1/4 cup
- **Almond Milk:** 1 cup, unsweetened
- **Greek Yogurt:** 1/2 cup, low-fat
- **Honey:** 1 tbsp (optional)
- **Ice Cubes:** 1 cup

Instructions:

1. **Blend Ingredients:**
   - Combine blueberries, rolled oats, almond milk, Greek yogurt, honey (if using), and ice cubes in a blender.
   - Blend until smooth.
2. **Serve:**
   - Pour into glasses and serve immediately.

8. Mango and Coconut Smoothie

Yield: 2 servings **Prepration time:** 5 Minutes **Cooking Time:** 0 Minutes

Nutritional Information (Per Serving):
- Calories: 150
- Protein: 2g
- Carbohydrates: 30g
- Fats: 4g
- Fiber: 3g
- Cholesterol: 0mg
- Sodium: 15mg
- Potassium: 350mg

Ingredients:

- **Mango:** 1, peeled and chopped
- **Coconut Milk:** 1 cup, unsweetened
- **Banana:** 1, sliced
- **Lime Juice:** 1 tbsp
- **Ice Cubes:** 1 cup

Instructions:

1. **Blend Ingredients:**
   - Combine mango, coconut milk, banana, lime juice, and ice cubes in a blender.
   - Blend until smooth.
2. **Serve:**
   - Pour into glasses and serve immediately.

9. Watermelon Mint Cooler

Yield: 4 servings Prepration time: 10 Minutes Cooking Time: 0 Minutes

Nutritional Information (Per Serving):
- **Calories:** 50
- **Protein:** 1g
- **Carbohydrates:** 12g
- **Fats:** 0.2g
- **Fiber:** 1g
- **Cholesterol:** 0mg
- **Sodium:** 2mg
- **Potassium:** 160mg

Ingredients:

- **Watermelon:** 4 cups, cubed
- **Lime Juice:** 2 tbsp
- **Mint Leaves:** 1/4 cup, chopped
- **Water:** 1 cup
- **Ice Cubes:** 1 cup

Instructions:

1. **Blend Ingredients:**
   - Combine watermelon, lime juice, mint leaves, water, and ice cubes in a blender.
   - Blend until smooth.
2. **Serve:**
   - Pour into glasses and serve immediately.

10. Carrot and Orange Juice

Yield: 2 servings Prepration time: 10 Minutes Cooking Time: 0 Minutes

Nutritional Information (Per Serving):
- **Calories:** 90
- **Protein:** 2g
- **Carbohydrates:** 22g
- **Fats:** 0.3g
- **Fiber:** 3g
- **Cholesterol:** 0mg
- **Sodium:** 45mg
- **Potassium:** 350mg

Ingredients:

- **Carrots:** 4, peeled and chopped
- **Oranges:** 2, peeled and segmented
- **Ginger:** 1 inch, peeled and grated
- **Water:** 1 cup

Instructions:

1. **Blend Ingredients:**
   - Combine carrots, oranges, ginger, and water in a blender.
   - Blend until smooth.
2. **Serve:**
   - Strain the juice through a fine-mesh sieve if desired.
   - Pour into glasses and serve immediately.

CHAPTER 11. STAPLES, SAUCES, DIPS, AND DRESSINGS

1. Low-Fat Ranch Dressing

- Yield: 1 cup (about 8 servings)
- Prepration time: 10 Minutes
- Cooking Time: 0 Minutes

Ingredients:

- **Greek Yogurt:** 1/2 cup, low-fat
- **Buttermilk:** 1/2 cup, low-fat
- **Garlic Powder:** 1/2 tsp
- **Onion Powder:** 1/2 tsp
- **Dried Dill:** 1 tsp
- **Dried Parsley:** 1 tsp
- **Salt:** 1/4 tsp
- **Black Pepper:** 1/4 tsp
- **Lemon Juice:** 1 tbsp

Nutritional Information (Per Serving):
- **Calories:** 30
- **Protein:** 2g
- **Carbohydrates:** 2g
- **Fats:** 1g
- **Fiber:** 0g
- **Cholesterol:** 5mg
- **Sodium:** 100mg
- **Potassium:** 100mg

Instructions:

1. **Mix Ingredients:**
   - In a bowl, combine Greek yogurt, buttermilk, garlic powder, onion powder, dried dill, dried parsley, salt, black pepper, and lemon juice.
2. **Whisk Until Smooth:**
   - Whisk until well combined and smooth.
3. **Serve:**
   - Serve immediately or refrigerate for up to a week.

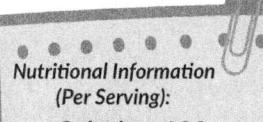

2. Avocado Cilantro Lime Dressing

Yield: 1 cup (about 8 servings) **Prepration time:** 10 Minutes **Cooking Time:** 0 Minutes

Ingredients:

- **Avocado:** 1, pitted and peeled
- **Cilantro:** 1/4 cup, fresh
- **Lime Juice:** 2 tbsp
- **Greek Yogurt:** 1/4 cup, low-fat
- **Olive Oil:** 2 tbsp
- **Garlic:** 1 clove, minced
- **Salt:** 1/4 tsp
- **Water:** 2-4 tbsp (to thin)

Nutritional Information (Per Serving):
- **Calories:** 60
- **Protein:** 1g
- **Carbohydrates:** 4g
- **Fats:** 5g
- **Fiber:** 2g
- **Cholesterol:** 0mg
- **Sodium:** 90mg
- **Potassium:** 150mg

Instructions:

1. **Blend Ingredients:**
   - In a blender, combine avocado, cilantro, lime juice, Greek yogurt, olive oil, garlic, salt, and water.
2. **Blend Until Smooth:**
   - Blend until smooth, adding more water if needed to reach desired consistency.
3. **Serve:**
   - Serve immediately or refrigerate for up to a week.

3. Roasted Red Pepper Hummus

Yield: 1 cup (about 8 servings) **Prepration time:** 10 Minutes **Cooking Time:** 0 Minutes

Ingredients:

- **Chickpeas:** 1 can (15 oz), drained and rinsed
- **Roasted Red Peppers:** 1 cup, chopped
- **Tahini:** 1/4 cup
- **Lemon Juice:** 2 tbsp
- **Garlic:** 2 cloves, minced
- **Olive Oil:** 2 tbsp
- **Cumin:** 1 tsp
- **Salt:** 1/2 tsp
- **Water:** 2-4 tbsp (to thin)

Nutritional Information (Per Serving):
- **Calories:** 100
- **Protein:** 3g
- **Carbohydrates:** 10g
- **Fats:** 5g
- **Fiber:** 3g
- **Cholesterol:** 0mg
- **Sodium:** 200mg
- **Potassium:** 140mg

Instructions:

1. **Blend Ingredients:**
   - In a blender or food processor, combine chickpeas, roasted red peppers, tahini, lemon juice, garlic, olive oil, cumin, salt, and water.
2. **Blend Until Smooth:**
   - Blend until smooth, adding more water if needed to reach desired consistency.
3. **Serve:**
   - Serve immediately or refrigerate for up to a week.

4. Tahini Lemon Sauce

Yield: 1 cup (about 8 servings) | **Prepration time:** 5 Minutes | **Cooking Time:** 0 Minutes

Ingredients:

- **Tahini:** 1/4 cup
- **Lemon Juice:** 1/4 cup
- **Garlic:** 1 clove, minced
- **Olive Oil:** 2 tbsp
- **Water:** 1/4 cup
- **Salt:** 1/4 tsp
- **Cumin:** 1/2 tsp

Nutritional Information (Per Serving):
- Calories: 70
- Protein: 2g
- Carbohydrates: 2g
- Fats: 6g
- Fiber: 1g
- Cholesterol: 0mg
- Sodium: 100mg
- Potassium: 60mg

Instructions:

1. **Mix Ingredients:**
   - In a bowl, whisk together tahini, lemon juice, garlic, olive oil, water, salt, and cumin.
2. **Whisk Until Smooth:**
   - Whisk until well combined and smooth.
3. **Serve:**
   - Serve immediately or refrigerate for up to a week.

5. Homemade Marinara Sauce

Yield: 4 cups (about 8 servings) | **Prepration time:** 10 Minutes | **Cooking Time:** 30 Minutes

Ingredients:

- **Olive Oil:** 2 tbsp
- **Onion:** 1, chopped
- **Garlic:** 4 cloves, minced
- **Crushed Tomatoes:** 2 cans (28 oz each)
- **Tomato Paste:** 2 tbsp
- **Dried Basil:** 1 tsp
- **Dried Oregano:** 1 tsp
- **Salt:** 1/2 tsp
- **Black Pepper:** 1/4 tsp

Nutritional Information (Per Serving):
- Calories: 60
- Protein: 2g
- Carbohydrates: 10g
- Fats: 2g
- Fiber: 3g
- Cholesterol: 0mg
- Sodium: 200mg
- Potassium: 400mg

Instructions:

1. **Cook Onions and Garlic:**
   - In a large pot, heat olive oil over medium heat.
   - Add chopped onion and cook for 5 minutes until softened.
   - Add minced garlic and cook for another 2 minutes.
2. **Add Tomatoes and Spices:**
   - Stir in crushed tomatoes, tomato paste, dried basil, dried oregano, salt, and black pepper.
   - Bring to a simmer and cook for 20-30 minutes, stirring occasionally.
3. **Serve:**
   - Serve immediately or store in the refrigerator for up to a week.

6. Greek Yogurt Tzatziki

Yield: 2 cups (about 8 servings) | Prepration time: 10 Minutes | Cooking Time: 0 Minutes

Ingredients:

- **Greek Yogurt:** 2 cups, low-fat
- **Cucumber:** 1, grated and drained
- **Garlic:** 2 cloves, minced
- **Lemon Juice:** 2 tbsp
- **Olive Oil:** 1 tbsp
- **Dill:** 1 tbsp, chopped
- **Salt:** 1/2 tsp
- **Black Pepper:** 1/4 tsp

Nutritional Information (Per Serving):
- **Calories:** 50
- **Protein:** 4g
- **Carbohydrates:** 4g
- **Fats:** 2g
- **Fiber:** 0.5g
- **Cholesterol:** 5mg
- **Sodium:** 150mg
- **Potassium:** 150mg

Instructions:

1. **Prepare Cucumber:**
   - Grate the cucumber and drain the excess liquid.
2. **Mix Ingredients:**
   - In a bowl, combine Greek yogurt, grated cucumber, minced garlic, lemon juice, olive oil, dill, salt, and black pepper.
3. **Stir Until Combined:**
   - Stir until well combined.
4. **Serve:**
   - Serve immediately or refrigerate for up to a week.

7. Balsamic Vinaigrette

Yield: 1 cup (about 8 servings) | Prepration time: 5 Minutes | Cooking Time: 0 Minutes

Ingredients:

- **Olive Oil:** 1/2 cup
- **Balsamic Vinegar:** 1/4 cup
- **Dijon Mustard:** 1 tbsp
- **Honey:** 1 tbsp
- **Garlic:** 1 clove, minced
- **Salt:** 1/4 tsp
- **Black Pepper:** 1/4 tsp

Nutritional Information (Per Serving):
- **Calories:** 100
- **Protein:** 0g
- **Carbohydrates:** 3g
- **Fats:** 10g
- **Fiber:** 0g
- **Cholesterol:** 0mg
- **Sodium:** 100mg
- **Potassium:** 20mg

Instructions:

1. **Mix Ingredients:**
   - In a bowl, whisk together olive oil, balsamic vinegar, Dijon mustard, honey, minced garlic, salt, and black pepper.
2. **Whisk Until Emulsified:**
   - Whisk until well combined and emulsified.
3. **Serve:**
   - Serve immediately or refrigerate for up to a week.

8. Spicy Sriracha Mayo

Yield: 1 cup (about 8 servings) | Prepration time: 5 Minutes | Cooking Time: 0 Minutes

Ingredients:

- **Greek Yogurt:** 1/2 cup, low-fat
- **Mayonnaise:** 1/4 cup, low-fat
- **Sriracha Sauce:** 2 tbsp
- **Lemon Juice:** 1 tbsp
- **Garlic Powder:** 1/2 tsp
- **Salt:** 1/4 tsp

Nutritional Information (Per Serving):
- **Calories:** 40
- **Protein:** 1g
- **Carbohydrates:** 1g
- **Fats:** 3g
- **Fiber:** 0g
- **Cholesterol:** 5mg
- **Sodium:** 150mg
- **Potassium:** 20mg

Instructions:

1. **Mix Ingredients:**
   - In a bowl, combine Greek yogurt, mayonnaise, sriracha sauce, lemon juice, garlic powder, and salt.
   - Stir until well combined.
2. **Serve:**
   - Serve immediately or refrigerate for up to a week.

9. Lemon Herb Aioli

Yield: 1 cup (about 8 servings) | Prepration time: 5 Minutes | Cooking Time: 0 Minutes

Ingredients:

- **Greek Yogurt:** 1/2 cup, low-fat
- **Mayonnaise:** 1/4 cup, low-fat
- **Lemon Juice:** 2 tbsp
- **Lemon Zest:** 1 tsp
- **Garlic:** 2 cloves, minced
- **Fresh Herbs (Parsley, Dill, Basil):** 2 tbsp, chopped
- **Salt:** 1/4 tsp
- **Black Pepper:** 1/4 tsp

Nutritional Information (Per Serving):
- **Calories:** 40
- **Protein:** 1g
- **Carbohydrates:** 1g
- **Fats:** 3g
- **Fiber:** 0g
- **Cholesterol:** 5mg
- **Sodium:** 120mg
- **Potassium:** 20mg

Instructions:

1. **Mix Ingredients:**
   - In a bowl, combine Greek yogurt, mayonnaise, lemon juice, lemon zest, minced garlic, fresh herbs, salt, and black pepper.
   - Stir until well combined.
2. **Serve:**
   - Serve immediately or refrigerate for up to a week.

10. Honey Mustard Dressing

🍽 Yield: 1 cup (about 8 servings)   ⏲ Prepration time: 5 Minutes   👨‍🍳 Cooking Time: 0 Minutes

Ingredients:

- **Greek Yogurt:** 1/2 cup, low-fat
- **Dijon Mustard:** 1/4 cup
- **Honey:** 2 tbsp
- **Apple Cider Vinegar:** 2 tbsp
- **Olive Oil:** 2 tbsp
- **Salt:** 1/4 tsp
- **Black Pepper:** 1/4 tsp

Nutritional Information (Per Serving):
- Calories: 60
- Protein: 1g
- Carbohydrates: 5g
- Fats: 4g
- Fiber: 0g
- Cholesterol: 0mg
- Sodium: 130mg
- Potassium: 30mg

Instructions:

1. **Mix Ingredients:**
   - In a bowl, combine Greek yogurt, Dijon mustard, honey, apple cider vinegar, olive oil, salt, and black pepper.
   - Whisk until smooth and well combined.
2. **Serve:**
   - Serve immediately or refrigerate for up to a week.

11. Garlic and Herb Quinoa

🍽 Yield: 4 servings   ⏲ Prepration time: 5 Minutes   👨‍🍳 Cooking Time: 15 Minutes

Ingredients:

- **Quinoa:** 1 cup, rinsed
- **Water or Low-Sodium Vegetable Broth:** 2 cups
- **Olive Oil:** 1 tbsp
- **Garlic:** 2 cloves, minced
- **Fresh Herbs (Parsley, Thyme, Basil):** 1/4 cup, chopped
- **Salt:** 1/2 tsp
- **Black Pepper:** 1/4 tsp

Nutritional Information (Per Serving):
- Calories: 150
- Protein: 5g
- Carbohydrates: 25g
- Fats: 4g
- Fiber: 3g
- Cholesterol: 0mg
- Sodium: 150mg
- Potassium: 250mg

Instructions:

1. **Cook Quinoa:**
   - In a saucepan, bring water or vegetable broth to a boil.
   - Add quinoa, reduce heat to low, cover, and simmer for 15 minutes until the quinoa is cooked and water is absorbed.
2. **Prepare Herb Mixture:**
   - In a small skillet, heat olive oil over medium heat.
   - Add minced garlic and cook for 1 minute until fragrant.
3. **Combine and Serve:**
   - Fluff the cooked quinoa with a fork and stir in the garlic, olive oil, fresh herbs, salt, and black pepper.
   - Serve warm.

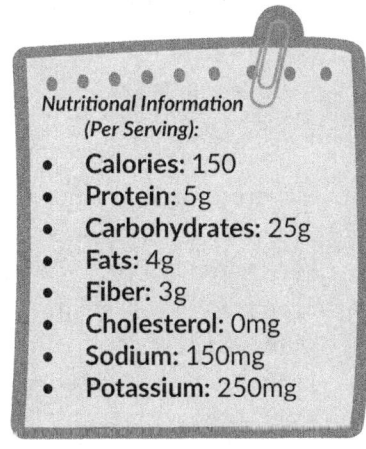

12. Chimichurri Sauce

Yield: 1 cup (about 8 servings) | **Prepration time:** 10 Minutes | **Cooking Time:** 0 Minutes

Ingredients:

- **Fresh Parsley:** 1 cup, packed
- **Fresh Cilantro:** 1/2 cup, packed
- **Garlic:** 3 cloves
- **Red Wine Vinegar:** 1/4 cup
- **Olive Oil:** 1/4 cup
- **Red Pepper Flakes:** 1/2 tsp
- **Salt:** 1/2 tsp
- **Black Pepper:** 1/4 tsp

Nutritional Information (Per Serving):
- **Calories:** 80
- **Protein:** 1g
- **Carbohydrates:** 2g
- **Fats:** 8g
- **Fiber:** 1g
- **Cholesterol:** 0mg
- **Sodium:** 150mg
- **Potassium:** 70mg

Instructions:

1. **Blend Ingredients:**
   - In a food processor, combine parsley, cilantro, garlic, red wine vinegar, olive oil, red pepper flakes, salt, and black pepper.
   - Pulse until well combined but still slightly chunky.
2. **Serve:**
   - Serve immediately or refrigerate for up to a week.

13. Mango Salsa

Yield: 2 cups (about 8 servings) | **Prepration time:** 10 Minutes | **Cooking Time:** 0 Minutes

Ingredients:

- **Mango:** 2, peeled and diced
- **Red Bell Pepper:** 1, diced
- **Red Onion:** 1/4 cup, finely chopped
- **Cilantro:** 1/4 cup, chopped
- **Lime Juice:** 2 tbsp
- **Jalapeño:** 1, seeded and minced (optional)
- **Salt:** 1/4 tsp

Nutritional Information (Per Serving):
- **Calories:** 40
- **Protein:** 1g
- **Carbohydrates:** 10g
- **Fats:** 0.2g
- **Fiber:** 2g
- **Cholesterol:** 0mg
- **Sodium:** 70mg
- **Potassium:** 150mg

Instructions:

1. **Mix Ingredients:**
   - In a bowl, combine diced mango, red bell pepper, red onion, cilantro, lime juice, jalapeño (if using), and salt.
   - Stir until well combined.
2. **Serve:**
   - Serve immediately or refrigerate for up to a week.

14. Peanut Sauce

- Yield: 1 cup (about 8 servings)
- Prepration time: 5 Minutes
- Cooking Time: 0 Minutes

Ingredients:

- **Peanut Butter:** 1/4 cup, natural
- **Soy Sauce:** 2 tbsp, low-sodium
- **Lime Juice:** 2 tbsp
- **Honey:** 1 tbsp
- **Garlic:** 2 cloves, minced
- **Ginger:** 1 tsp, grated
- **Water:** 1/4 cup (to thin)

Nutritional Information (Per Serving):
- Calories: 70
- Protein: 2g
- Carbohydrates: 4g
- Fats: 5g
- Fiber: 1g
- Cholesterol: 0mg
- Sodium: 170mg
- Potassium: 70mg

Instructions:

1. **Mix Ingredients:**
   - In a bowl, combine peanut butter, soy sauce, lime juice, honey, minced garlic, grated ginger, and water.
   - Whisk until smooth and well combined.
2. **Serve:**
   - Serve immediately or refrigerate for up to a week.

15. Pesto with Spinach and Basil

- Yield: 1 cup (about 8 servings)
- Prepration time: 10 Minutes
- Cooking Time: 0 Minutes

Ingredients:

- **Fresh Spinach:** 1 cup, packed
- **Fresh Basil:** 1 cup, packed
- **Pine Nuts:** 1/4 cup
- **Parmesan Cheese:** 1/4 cup, grated
- **Garlic:** 2 cloves
- **Lemon Juice:** 2 tbsp
- **Olive Oil:** 1/4 cup
- **Salt:** 1/4 tsp
- **Black Pepper:** 1/4 tsp

Nutritional Information (Per Serving):
- Calories: 100
- Protein: 3g
- Carbohydrates: 2g
- Fats: 9g
- Fiber: 1g
- Cholesterol: 5mg
- Sodium: 120mg
- Potassium: 120mg

Instructions:

1. **Blend Ingredients:**
   - In a food processor, combine spinach, basil, pine nuts, Parmesan cheese, garlic, lemon juice, olive oil, salt, and black pepper.
   - Blend until smooth.
2. **Serve:**
   - Serve immediately or refrigerate for up to a week.

45-DAY MEAL PLAN

Week 1

Day 1:
- **Breakfast:** Avocado and Spinach Breakfast Wrap
- **Snack:** Spicy Hummus and Veggie Sticks
- **Lunch:** Grilled Lemon Herb Salmon
- **Dinner:** Grilled Chicken and Vegetable Skewers

Day 2:
- **Breakfast:** Quinoa and Berry Breakfast Bowl
- **Snack:** Baked Kale Chips
- **Lunch:** Mediterranean Quinoa Salad
- **Dinner:** Turkey and Spinach Meatballs

Day 3:
- **Breakfast:** Egg White Veggie Omelette
- **Snack:** Quinoa-Stuffed Mini Bell Peppers
- **Lunch:** Chicken and Avocado Salad
- **Dinner:** Lemon Herb Roasted Chicken

Day 4:
- **Breakfast:** Whole Grain Banana Pancakes
- **Snack:** Cucumber and Dill Greek Yogurt Dip
- **Lunch:** Chickpea and Spinach Soup
- **Dinner:** Baked Cod with Garlic and Herbs

Day 5:
- **Breakfast:** Chia Seed Pudding with Fresh Berries
- **Snack:** Sweet Potato and Black Bean Bites
- **Lunch:** Butternut Squash Soup
- **Dinner:** Slow-Cooked Beef and Veggie Stew

Day 6:
- **Breakfast:** Low-Fat Greek Yogurt Parfait
- **Snack:** Almond-Crusted Zucchini Fries
- **Lunch:** Spinach and Strawberry Salad
- **Dinner:** Seared Tuna with Mango Salsa

Day 7:
- **Breakfast:** Almond Butter and Banana Smoothie Bowl
- **Snack:** Roasted Red Pepper and Walnut Dip
- **Lunch:** Sweet Potato and Kale Hash
- **Dinner:** Coconut Crusted Tilapia

Week 1 Shopping List:

Produce:
- Avocado
- Spinach
- Berries (blueberries, strawberries, etc.)
- Apples
- Bananas
- Sweet potatoes
- Kale
- Zucchini
- Mushrooms
- Tomatoes
- Red peppers
- Lemon
- Herbs (cilantro, parsley, etc.)

Protein:
- Salmon fillets
- Chicken breasts
- Turkey
- Beef (lean cuts)
- Shrimp
- Eggs
- Greek yogurt

Grains & Legumes:
- Quinoa
- Whole grain bread
- Whole wheat tortillas
- Oatmeal
- Black beans
- Chickpeas

Dairy & Dairy Substitutes:
- Low-fat Greek yogurt
- Cottage cheese
- Almond milk

Pantry Staples:
- Olive oil
- Honey
- Balsamic vinegar
- Dijon mustard
- Salsa
- Soy sauce
- Garlic
- Spices (cumin, paprika, etc.)

Nuts & Seeds:
- Almonds
- Chia seeds
- Flaxseeds

Week 2

Day 8:
- **Breakfast:** Oatmeal with Fresh Apples and Cinnamon
- **Snack:** Low-Fat Spinach Artichoke Dip
- **Lunch:** Greek Salad with Low-Fat Feta
- **Dinner:** Chicken and Quinoa Stuffed Peppers

Day 9:
- **Breakfast:** Veggie-Packed Breakfast Frittata
- **Snack:** Edamame and Sea Salt
- **Lunch:** Tomato Basil Soup
- **Dinner:** Shrimp and Avocado Salad

Day 10:
- **Breakfast:** Smoked Salmon and Avocado Toast
- **Snack:** Avocado and Tomato Bruschetta
- **Lunch:** Lentil and Vegetable Stew
- **Dinner:** Ginger Beef Stir-Fry

Day 11:
- **Breakfast:** Blueberry Almond Overnight Oats
- **Snack:** Spicy Hummus and Veggie Sticks
- **Lunch:** Mediterranean Baked Halibut
- **Dinner:** Teriyaki Chicken and Vegetable Stir-Fry

Day 12:
- **Breakfast:** Spinach and Mushroom Breakfast Tacos
- **Snack:** Baked Kale Chips
- **Lunch:** Chickpea and Tomato Salad
- **Dinner:** Turkey and Sweet Potato Chili

Day 13:
- **Breakfast:** Baked Sweet Potato and Black Bean Breakfast Skillet
- **Snack:** Quinoa-Stuffed Mini Bell Peppers
- **Lunch:** Greek-Style Stuffed Tomatoes
- **Dinner:** Garlic Shrimp and Asparagus Stir-Fry

Day 14:
- **Breakfast:** Low-Fat Cottage Cheese and Fresh Fruit
- **Snack:** Cucumber and Dill Greek Yogurt Dip
- **Lunch:** Wild Rice and Mushroom Soup
- **Dinner:** Honey Mustard Baked Chicken Thighs

Week 2 Shopping List:

Produce:
- Avocado
- Spinach
- Mushrooms
- Apples
- Berries
- Tomatoes
- Zucchini
- Lemon
- Kale
- Carrots

Protein:
- Salmon fillets
- Chicken breasts
- Turkey breasts
- Shrimp
- Greek yogurt
- Cottage cheese

Grains & Legumes:
- Quinoa
- Black beans
- Chickpeas

Dairy & Dairy Substitutes:
- Low-fat Greek yogurt
- Cottage cheese

Pantry Staples:
- Olive oil
- Coconut oil
- Honey
- Dijon mustard
- Balsamic vinegar
- Spices (cumin, paprika, etc.)

Nuts & Seeds:
- Almonds
- Chia seeds
- Flaxseeds

Week 3

Day 15:
- **Breakfast:** Turkey and Avocado Breakfast Sandwich
- **Snack:** Almond-Crusted Zucchini Fries
- **Lunch:** Spinach and Feta Stuffed Portobello Mushrooms
- **Dinner:** Grilled Lemon Herb Chicken Thighs

Day 16:
- **Breakfast:** Apple Cinnamon Quinoa Porridge
- **Snack:** Roasted Red Pepper and Walnut Dip
- **Lunch:** Kale and Apple Slaw
- **Dinner:** Lemon Garlic Chicken Breasts

Day 17:
- **Breakfast:** Savory Oatmeal with Poached Egg
- **Snack:** Low-Fat Spinach Artichoke Dip
- **Lunch:** Spicy Pumpkin Soup
- **Dinner:** Beef and Broccoli Stir-Fry

Day 18:
- **Breakfast:** Whole Wheat English Muffin with Tomato and Basil
- **Snack:** Edamame and Sea Salt
- **Lunch:** Spicy Turkey Lettuce Wraps
- **Dinner:** Blackened Mahi Mahi

Day 19:
- **Breakfast:** Green Smoothie with Kale and Pineapple
- **Snack:** Avocado and Tomato Bruschetta
- **Lunch:** Cauliflower and Leek Soup
- **Dinner:** Grilled Shrimp with Pineapple Salsa

Day 20:
- **Breakfast:** Ricotta and Berry Stuffed French Toast
- **Snack:** Roasted Chickpeas with Paprika
- **Lunch:** Mediterranean Tuna Stuffed Tomatoes
- **Dinner:** Beef and Mushroom Lettuce Wraps

Day 21:
- **Breakfast:** Zucchini and Carrot Breakfast Muffins
- **Snack:** Fresh Spring Rolls with Peanut Dipping Sauce
- **Lunch:** Baked Ratatouille
- **Dinner:** Garlic Shrimp and Asparagus Stir-Fry

Week 3 Shopping List:

Produce:
- Avocado
- Spinach
- Zucchini
- Carrots
- Berries (blueberries, strawberries, etc.)
- Apples
- Kale
- Pineapple
- Mushrooms
- Leeks
- Tomatoes
- Lemon
- Herbs (basil, parsley, cilantro)
- Portobello mushrooms
- Bell peppers
- Garlic

Protein:
- Chicken breasts
- Turkey
- Shrimp
- Beef (lean cuts)
- Eggs
- Ricotta cheese
- Greek yogurt

Grains & Legumes:
- Quinoa
- Whole wheat English muffins
- Black beans
- Chickpeas

Dairy & Dairy Substitutes:
- Low-fat Greek yogurt
- Ricotta cheese

Pantry Staples:
- Olive oil
- Balsamic vinegar
- Dijon mustard
- Salsa
- Peanut butter
- Soy sauce
- Spices (cumin, paprika, etc.)

Nuts & Seeds:
- Almonds
- Flaxseeds

Week 4

Day 22:
- **Breakfast:** Low-Fat Greek Yogurt and Granola Bowl
- **Snack:** Smoked Salmon and Cucumber Bites
- **Lunch:** Moroccan Lentil Soup
- **Dinner:** Herb-Crusted Roast Beef

Day 23:
- **Breakfast:** Sweet Potato and Spinach Hash
- **Snack:** Baked Apple Chips with Cinnamon
- **Lunch:** Chicken and Avocado Salad
- **Dinner:** Lemon Dill Baked Salmon

Day 24:
- **Breakfast:** Low-Fat Cottage Cheese and Tomato Toast
- **Snack:** Mini Caprese Skewers
- **Lunch:** Roasted Beet and Arugula Salad
- **Dinner:** Beef and Vegetable Stuffed Bell Peppers

Day 25:
- **Breakfast:** Tofu Scramble with Spinach and Mushrooms
- **Snack:** Roasted Chickpeas with Paprika
- **Lunch:** Sweet Potato and Black Bean Soup
- **Dinner:** Grilled Chicken Caesar Salad

Day 26:
- **Breakfast:** Lemon Poppy Seed Protein Pancakes
- **Snack:** Avocado Deviled Eggs
- **Lunch:** Lentil and Spinach Stuffed Acorn Squash
- **Dinner:** Parchment-Baked Cod with Vegetables

Day 27:
- **Breakfast:** Baked Eggs in Avocado
- **Snack:** Cucumber and Dill Greek Yogurt Dip
- **Lunch:** Broccoli and Kale Soup
- **Dinner:** Spaghetti Squash with Marinara Sauce

Day 28:
- **Breakfast:** Mango and Coconut Chia Pudding
- **Snack:** Fresh Spring Rolls with Peanut Dipping Sauce
- **Lunch:** Arugula and Beet Salad
- **Dinner:** Chicken and Zucchini Noodles

Week 4 Shopping List:

Produce:
- Avocado
- Spinach
- Mushrooms
- Berries (blueberries, strawberries, etc.)
- Sweet potatoes
- Kale
- Beets
- Zucchini
- Cucumbers
- Tomatoes
- Broccoli
- Arugula
- Lemon
- Mango
- Bell peppers
- Garlic
- Acorn squash

Protein:
- Chicken breasts
- Beef (lean cuts)
- Salmon
- Cod
- Tofu
- Eggs
- Cottage cheese
- Greek yogurt
- Smoked salmon

Grains & Legumes:
- Quinoa
- Whole wheat English muffins
- Black beans
- Lentils
- Chickpeas

Dairy & Dairy Substitutes:
- Low-fat Greek yogurt
- Cottage cheese
- Almond milk
- Pantry Staples:
- Olive oil
- Balsamic vinegar
- Dijon mustard
- Peanut butter

- » Soy sauce
- » Spices (cumin, paprika, etc.)

Nuts & Seeds:
- » Almonds
- » Chia seeds
- » Flaxseeds

Week 5

Day 29:
- **Breakfast:** Spinach and Feta Stuffed Breakfast Wrap
- **Snack:** Baked Cauliflower Buffalo Bites
- **Lunch:** Chicken and Avocado Salad
- **Dinner:** Grilled Lemon Herb Salmon

Day 30:
- **Breakfast:** Whole Grain Waffles with Berry Compote
- **Snack:** Greek Yogurt Ranch Dip with Carrot Sticks
- **Lunch:** Mediterranean Quinoa Salad
- **Dinner:** Turkey and Spinach Meatballs

Day 31:
- **Breakfast:** Baked Sweet Potato and Black Bean Breakfast Skillet
- **Snack:** Almond-Crusted Zucchini Fries
- **Lunch:** Tomato Basil Soup
- **Dinner:** Teriyaki Chicken and Vegetable Stir-Fry

Day 32:
- **Breakfast:** Low-Fat Greek Yogurt Parfait
- **Snack:** Edamame and Sea Salt
- **Lunch:** Sweet Potato and Kale Hash
- **Dinner:** Blackened Mahi Mahi

Day 33:
- **Breakfast:** Almond Butter and Banana Smoothie Bowl
- **Snack:** Roasted Red Pepper and Walnut Dip
- **Lunch:** Greek Salad with Low-Fat Feta
- **Dinner:** Slow-Cooked Beef and Veggie Stew

Day 34:
- **Breakfast:** Oatmeal with Fresh Apples and Cinnamon
- **Snack:** Low-Fat Spinach Artichoke Dip
- **Lunch:** Lentil and Spinach Stuffed Acorn Squash
- **Dinner:** Beef and Broccoli Stir-Fry

Day 35:
- **Breakfast:** Veggie-Packed Breakfast Frittata
- **Snack:** Fresh Spring Rolls with Peanut Dipping Sauce
- **Lunch:** Chickpea and Tomato Salad
- **Dinner:** Shrimp and Avocado Salad

Week 5 Shopping List:

Produce:
- Avocado
- Spinach
- Berries (blueberries, strawberries, etc.)
- Sweet potatoes
- Kale
- Tomatoes
- Zucchini
- Cucumbers
- Broccoli
- Arugula
- Apples
- Carrots
- Cauliflower
- Bell peppers
- Garlic

Protein:
- Chicken breasts
- Turkey
- Beef (lean cuts)
- Salmon
- Shrimp
- Eggs
- Greek yogurt
- Feta cheese

Grains & Legumes:
- Quinoa
- Whole grain waffles
- Black beans
- Lentils
- Chickpeas

Dairy & Dairy Substitutes:
- Low-fat Greek yogurt
- Almond milk

Pantry Staples:
- Olive oil
- Balsamic vinegar
- Dijon mustard
- Peanut butter
- Soy sauce
- Spices (cumin, paprika, etc.)

Nuts & Seeds:
- Almonds
- Flaxseeds

Week 6

Day 36:
- **Breakfast:** Smoked Salmon and Avocado Toast
- **Snack:** Mini Caprese Skewers
- **Lunch:** Arugula and Beet Salad
- **Dinner:** Chicken and Zucchini Noodles

Day 37:
- **Breakfast:** Blueberry Almond Overnight Oats
- **Snack:** Baked Kale Chips
- **Lunch:** Roasted Red Pepper and Tomato Soup
- **Dinner:** Herb-Crusted Roast Beef

Day 38:
- **Breakfast:** Spinach and Mushroom Breakfast Tacos
- **Snack:** Cucumber and Dill Greek Yogurt Dip
- **Lunch:** Sweet Potato and Black Bean Soup
- **Dinner:** Beef and Mushroom Lettuce Wraps

Day 39:
- **Breakfast:** Baked Sweet Potato and Black Bean Breakfast Skillet
- **Snack:** Spicy Hummus and Veggie Sticks
- **Lunch:** Mediterranean Baked Halibut
- **Dinner:** Ginger Beef Stir-Fry

Day 40:
- **Breakfast:** Low-Fat Cottage Cheese and Fresh Fruit
- **Snack:** Almond-Crusted Zucchini Fries
- **Lunch:** Grilled Lemon Herb Chicken Thighs
- **Dinner:** Parchment-Baked Cod with Vegetables

Day 41:
- **Breakfast:** Tofu Scramble with Spinach and Mushrooms
- **Snack:** Roasted Red Pepper and Walnut Dip
- **Lunch:** Classic Minestrone
- **Dinner:** Teriyaki Chicken and Vegetable Stir-Fry

Day 42:
- **Breakfast:** Lemon Poppy Seed Protein Pancakes
- **Snack:** Edamame and Sea Salt
- **Lunch:** Kale and Apple Slaw
- **Dinner:** Blackened Mahi Mahi

Week 6 Shopping List:

Produce:
- Avocado
- Spinach
- Mushrooms
- Berries (blueberries, strawberries, etc.)
- Sweet potatoes
- Kale
- Beets
- Zucchini
- Cucumbers
- Tomatoes
- Broccoli
- Arugula
- Apples
- Bell peppers
- Garlic

Protein:
- Chicken breasts
- Beef (lean cuts)
- Salmon
- Cod
- Tofu
- Eggs
- Cottage cheese
- Smoked salmon

Grains & Legumes:
- Quinoa
- Whole wheat bread
- Black beans
- Lentils
- Chickpeas

Dairy & Dairy Substitutes:
- Low-fat Greek yogurt
- Cottage cheese
- Almond milk

Pantry Staples:
- Olive oil
- Balsamic vinegar
- Dijon mustard
- Peanut butter
- Soy sauce
- Spices (cumin, paprika, etc.)

Nuts & Seeds:
- Almonds
- Flaxseeds

Week 7

Day 43:
- **Breakfast:** Baked Eggs in Avocado
- **Snack:** Roasted Chickpeas with Paprika
- **Lunch:** Spinach and Strawberry Salad
- **Dinner:** Grilled Shrimp with Pineapple Salsa

Day 44:
- **Breakfast:** Mango and Coconut Chia Pudding
- **Snack:** Fresh Spring Rolls with Peanut Dipping Sauce
- **Lunch:** Arugula and Beet Salad
- **Dinner:** Herb-Crusted Roast Beef

Day 45:
- **Breakfast:** Whole Wheat English Muffin with Tomato and Basil
- **Snack:** Baked Kale Chips
- **Lunch:** Greek Salad with Low-Fat Feta
- **Dinner:** Grilled Chicken Caesar Salad

Week 7 Shopping List:

Produce:
- Avocado
- Spinach
- Strawberries
- Mango
- Beets
- Pineapple
- Zucchini
- Cucumbers
- Tomatoes
- Arugula
- Lemon
- Herbs (basil, parsley, cilantro)
- Bell peppers
- Garlic

Protein:
- Chicken breasts
- Shrimp
- Beef (lean cuts)
- Eggs
- Feta cheese

Grains & Legumes:
- Whole wheat English muffins
- Quinoa
- Chickpeas

Dairy & Dairy Substitutes:
- Low-fat Greek yogurt
- Almond milk

Pantry Staples:
- Olive oil
- Balsamic vinegar
- Dijon mustard
- Peanut butter
- Soy sauce
- Spices (cumin, paprika, etc.)

Nuts & Seeds:
- Almonds
- Chia seeds
- Flaxseeds

APPENDIX 1. MEASUREMENT CONVERSION CHART

Weight Conversions

Imperial (oz)	Metric (g)	Imperial (oz)	Metric (g)
1/2 oz	14 g	9 oz	255 g
1 oz	28 g	10 oz	284 g
2 oz	57 g	11 oz	312 g
3 oz	85 g	12 oz	340 g
4 oz (1/4 lb)	113 g	13 oz	369 g
5 oz	142 g	14 oz	397 g
6 oz	170 g	15 oz	425 g
7 oz	198 g	16 oz (1 lb)	454 g
8 oz (1/2 lb)	227 g		

Volume Conversions

Cups	Fluid Ounces (fl oz)	Milliliters (ml)	Tablespoons (tbsp)
1/16 cup	1 fl oz	30 ml	2 tbsp
1/8 cup	1 fl oz	30 ml	2 tbsp
1/4 cup	2 fl oz	60 ml	4 tbsp
1/3 cup	2.67 fl oz	80 ml	5 tbsp + 1 tsp
1/2 cup	4 fl oz	120 ml	8 tbsp
2/3 cup	5.33 fl oz	160 ml	10 tbsp + 2 tsp
3/4 cup	6 fl oz	180 ml	12 tbsp
1 cup	8 fl oz	240 ml	16 tbsp
1 1/2 cup	12 fl oz	360 ml	24 tbsp
2 cups	16 fl oz	480 ml	32 tbsp
3 cups	24 fl oz	720 ml	48 tbsp
4 cups	32 fl oz	960 ml	64 tbsp
5 cups	40 fl oz	1200 ml	80 tbsp
6 cups	48 fl oz	1440 ml	96 tbsp
7 cups	56 fl oz	1680 ml	112 tbsp
8 cups	64 fl oz	1920 ml	128 tbsp

Temperature Conversions

Fahrenheit (°F)	Celsius (°C)	Fahrenheit (°F)	Celsius (°C)
100°F	38°C	330°F	166°C
110°F	43°C	340°F	171°C
120°F	49°C	350°F	177°C
130°F	54°C	360°F	182°C
140°F	60°C	370°F	188°C
150°F	66°C	380°F	193°C
160°F	71°C	390°F	199°C
170°F	77°C	400°F	204°C
180°F	82°C	410°F	210°C
190°F	88°C	420°F	216°C
200°F	93°C	430°F	221°C
210°F	99°C	440°F	227°C
220°F	104°C	450°F	232°C
230°F	110°C	460°F	238°C
240°F	116°C	470°F	243°C
250°F	121°C	480°F	249°C
260°F	127°C	490°F	254°C
270°F	132°C	500°F	260°C
280°F	138°C	510°F	266°C
290°F	143°C	520°F	271°C
300°F	149°C	530°F	277°C
310°F	154°C	540°F	282°C
320°F	160°C	550°F	288°C

APPENDIX 2. RECIPE INDEX

A

Almond Butter and Banana Smoothie 148
Almond Butter and Banana Smoothie Bowl 17
Almond-Crusted Zucchini Fries 36
Almond Flour Blueberry Muffins 133
Apple Cinnamon Quinoa Bake 139
Apple Cinnamon Quinoa Porridge 26
Arugula and Beet Salad 108
Avocado and Spinach Breakfast Wrap 11
Avocado and Tomato Bruschetta 40
Avocado Chocolate Mousse 131
Avocado Cilantro Lime Dressing 152

B

Baked Cod with Garlic and Herbs 42
Baked Kale Chips 32
Baked Ratatouille 121
Baked Sweet Potato and Black Bean Breakfast-Skillet 23
Baked Turkey Meatloaf 69
Balsamic Glazed Carrots 78
Balsamic Vinaigrette 154
BBQ Chicken and Pineapple Kebabs 63
Beef and Broccoli Stir-Fry 66
Beef and Mushroom Lettuce Wraps 75
Beef and Vegetable Stuffed Bell Peppers 70
Berry Chia Seed Pudding 132
Berry Protein Shake 146
Black Bean and Corn Salad 107
Black Bean and Corn Stuffed Sweet Potatoes 128
Blackened Mahi Mahi 54
Blueberry Almond Overnight Oats 21
Blueberry and Lemon Zest Greek Yogurt Bars 145
Blueberry and Oat Smoothie 149
Butternut Squash and Sage Risotto 123
Butternut Squash Soup 94

C

Carrot and Orange Juice 150
Carrot Cake Energy Bites 137
Carrot Ginger Soup 99
Cauliflower and Leek Soup 97
Cauliflower Chickpea Tacos 118
Cauliflower Rice Pilaf 79
Chia Seed and Coconut Pudding 140
Chia Seed Lemonade 148
Chia Seed Pudding with Fresh Berries 15
Chicken and Avocado Salad 102
Chicken and Quinoa Stuffed Peppers 61
Chicken and Zucchini Noodles 71
Chickpea and Spinach Soup 92
Chickpea and Tomato Salad 85
Chickpea and Vegetable Curry 113
Chimichurri Sauce 157
Chocolate Avocado Brownies 144
Classic Minestrone 95
Coconut Crusted Tilapia 47
Coconut Milk Panna Cotta 134
Coconut Water and Pineapple Cooler 147
Cucumber and Dill Greek Yogurt Dip 34
Cucumber and Dill Salad 90, 109

E

Edamame and Sea Salt 39
Eggplant Parmesan 114
Egg White Veggie Omelette 13

G

Garlic and Herb Quinoa 156
Garlic Roasted Brussels Sprouts 76
Garlic Shrimp and Asparagus Stir-Fry 48
Ginger Beef Stir-Fry 62
Greek Salad with Low-Fat Feta 105
Greek-Style Stuffed Tomatoes 125
Greek Yogurt Tzatziki 154
Green Detox Smoothie 146
Green Smoothie with Kale and Pineapple 29
Grilled Chicken and Vegetable Skewers 56
Grilled Chicken Caesar Salad 73
Grilled Lemon Herb Salmon 41
Grilled Shrimp with Pineapple Salsa 55
Grilled Vegetable and Hummus Wraps 127
Grilled Vegetable Medley 84

H

Herb-Crusted Roast Beef 72
Homemade Marinara Sauce 153
Honey Mustard Baked Chicken Thighs 67
Honey Mustard Dressing 156

K

Kale and Apple Slaw 103

L

Lemon Dill Baked Salmon 51
Lemon Garlic Asparagus 83
Lemon Garlic Chicken Breasts 64
Lemon Herb Aioli 155
Lemon Herb Roasted Chicken 58
Lemon Yogurt Parfaits 136
Lentil and Spinach Stuffed Acorn Squash 117
Lentil and Vegetable Stew 93
Lentil Shepherd's Pie 126

Low-Fat Cottage Cheese and Fresh Fruit 24
Low-Fat Greek Yogurt Parfait 16
Low-Fat Ranch Dressing 151
Low-Fat Spinach Artichoke Dip 38

M

Mango and Coconut Smoothie 149
Mango Salsa 157
Mango Sorbet 138
Mediterranean Baked Halibut 49
Mediterranean Quinoa Salad 101
Mixed Greens with Berries and Walnuts 110
Mushroom and Spinach Lasagna 124

O

Oatmeal Raisin Cookies 135
Oatmeal with Fresh Apples and Cinnamon - (continued) 18

P

Parchment-Baked Cod with Vegetables 53
Peanut Sauce 158
Pesto with Spinach and Basil 158
Pineapple and Coconut Ice Pops 143
Portobello Mushroom Burgers 115

Q

Quinoa and Berry Breakfast Bowl 12
Quinoa and Black Bean Salad 77
Quinoa and Vegetable Stuffed Zucchini Boats 122
Quinoa-Stuffed Mini Bell Peppers 33

R

Raspberry and Almond Crumble 142
Ricotta and Berry Stuffed French Toast 30
Roasted Beet and Arugula Salad 82
Roasted Butternut Squash with Sage 88
Roasted Red Pepper and Tomato Soup 96
Roasted Red Pepper and Walnut Dip 37
Roasted Red Pepper Hummus 152

S

Salmon and Quinoa Patties 50
Sautéed Spinach with Garlic 80
Savory Oatmeal with Poached Egg 27

Seared Tuna with Mango Salsa 44
Sesame Chicken and Broccoli 74
Shrimp and Avocado Salad 43
Shrimp and Vegetable Skewers 52
Slow-Cooked Beef and Veggie Stew 59
Smoked Salmon and Avocado Toast 20
Spaghetti Squash with Marinara Sauce 86, 112
Spicy Fish Tacos with Cabbage Slaw 45
Spicy Hummus and Veggie Sticks 31
Spicy Sriracha Mayo 155
Spicy Turkey Lettuce Wraps 60
Spinach and Avocado Smoothie 147
Spinach and Feta Stuffed Portobello Mushrooms 130
Spinach and Mushroom Breakfast Tacos 22
Spinach and Strawberry Salad 106
Steamed Broccoli with Lemon Zest 87
Steamed Mussels in White Wine Sauce 46
Stuffed Bell Peppers with Quinoa and Black Beans 111
Sweet Potato and Black Bean Bites 35
Sweet Potato and Black Bean Enchiladas 116
Sweet Potato and Black Bean Soup 100
Sweet Potato and Kale Hash 81

T

Tahini Lemon Sauce 153
Teriyaki Chicken and Vegetable Stir-Fry 68
Thai-Inspired Shrimp Salad 104
Tomato Basil Soup 91
Turkey and Avocado Breakfast Sandwich 25
Turkey and Spinach Meatballs 57
Turkey and Sweet Potato Chili 65

V

Vegan Banana Bread 141
Vegetable Stir-Fry with Tofu 120
Veggie-Packed Breakfast Frittata (continued) 19
Veggie-Packed Buddha Bowl 129

W

Watermelon Mint Cooler 150
Whole Grain Banana Pancakes 14
Whole Wheat English Muffin with Tomato and Basil 28
Wild Rice and Mushroom Soup 98

Z

Zucchini Noodles with Pesto 89, 119

We value your feedback!

Please leave an honest review to help us improve and assist others in their healthy journey!

Thank you!

Printed in Great Britain
by Amazon